Evaluating
Teaching

Evaluating Teaching

Kenneth O. Doyle, Jr.

LexingtonBooks
D.C. Heath and Company
Lexington, Massachusetts
Toronto

Library of Congress Cataloging in Publication Data

Doyle, Kenneth O.
  Evaluating teaching.

  Bibliography: p.
  Includes index.
  1. Teachers—Rating of.   2. Teaching—Evaluation.   I. Title.
LB2838.D69   1982   371.1'44   79-9673
ISBN 0-669-03613-7

Second printing, February 1984

Published simultaneously in Canada

Printed in the United States of America

International Standard Book Number: 0-669-03613-7

Library of Congress Catalog Card Number: 79-9673

MacKenzie

Contents

Figures and Table

Table

Preface and Acknowledgments

Ten years ago, dissertation fresh in hand, I innocently believed that I could meet my responsibility for devising an instructional-evaluation program for the University of Minnesota by the straightforward application of psychometric principles—reliability, validity, item analysis, and so forth—to questionnaires, rating scales, and tests. I discovered, perhaps more slowly than I should admit, that psychometrics supplies less than a total solution to the problem of evaluating teaching. A more rounded, more realistic plan for evaluating teaching would profit from knowledge about such diverse fields as rhetoric and communications, philosophy and philosophy of science, statistics, computer science, law, sociology and anthropology, business, graphic arts, and many of the subfields of psychology—social, clinical, organizational, personality, experimental, and differential. Each of these disciplines, and probably others, bears importantly on the collection, analysis, interpretation, or use of evaluative information. I have surely not exploited what all of these fields have to offer, but I have tried to touch on each of them, despite the psychometric orientation of this book. Perhaps later authors will elaborate where I have been able only to acknowledge a potential contribution.

I discovered further that, while the psychometrics of achievement testing is well advanced and sometimes even elegant, the psychometrics of questionnaires and rating scales is comparatively primitive, especially with respect to why people perceive each other as they do and how they arrive at and communicate those perceptions. Although I am certainly not competent to offer a new theory of evaluation, person-perception, or instrumentation, I am willing, in the spirit of Clark Hull, to take the risk of outlining some ideas that, wise or foolish, may eventually help in understanding the evaluation of teaching.

I noticed also that not everyone thinks of instructional evaluation as an altogether constructive enterprise. Despite the occasional ferocity of debate about evaluation policies, principles, and practices, it is clear that the majority of combatants are sincere and thoughtful people. Indeed, it may be that a portion of the vigor with which evaluation is sometimes discussed rises from lack of information and a portion from outrageous statements now and then offered by the proponents or opponents of one or another aspect of evaluation. I am convinced that instructional evaluation is constructive, and I have tried to be informative and only sometimes outrageous.

It has become clear that there are two kinds of people in the world, normal faculty, administrators, and students—and evaluation experts. Despite reciprocal suspiciousness, the similarities between these two groups may be greater than the differences, in that people in both groups are usually trying to understand and solve the same problems, although the words they use may be different. I have tried to address what I think are the major mutual concerns and to do so in a common language.

I have continually been annoyed by the fundamental inequity of scrutinizing some kinds of information—for example, student evaluations—while assuming the quality of other information—for example, colleague evaluations, self-evaluations, and tests. Consequently, I have tried to develop criteria for data and to apply those criteria in the same ways to all kinds of evaluation data. In this respect, my cubic schemata have been a very useful source of discipline and structure.

One of the few things of which I am sure is the debt I owe to my friends and colleagues for much of my thinking about instructional evaluation. The faculty and students at Mount St. Paul's, the Gregorian, and Marquette University bear some responsibility for the humanistic and philosophical values that I hope have influenced my thinking. My colleagues in the American Educational Research Association Special Interest Group on Instructional Evaluation and the Committee on Institutional Cooperation Panel on Faculty Evaluation and Development have helped me to merge those softer qualities into what I hope is a rigorous evaluation framework. My colleagues at the University of Minnesota Measurement Services Center, Department of Psychology, and Department of Educational Psychology, especially Darwin Hendel, Ross Moen, Tom Trabin, Susan Whitely, Dave Weiss, and Clyde Parker, have both stimulated me and tried to keep me sane. Gisele Nelson, Lenore Bergin, and Cathy Bennetts took much of the burden of this manuscript from me. Finally, my wife and our daughter have continually reminded me about what is really important. To all of them, my gratitude.

Part I:
Perspective

1

History of
Instructional Evaluation

In Antioch in about 350 A.D. any father who felt dissatisfied with the performance of the teacher in whose care he had placed his son had the privilege of examining the boy, or having him examined by competent authority, to determine whether the teacher might have been neglecting his duty. If the examination indicated that the teacher had indeed been neglectful, the father could enter a formal complaint against the teacher and have the case tried by a panel of teachers and laymen. Should the trial confirm the teacher's negligence, the father would be permitted to transfer his son—along with his patronage and fees—to another teacher. This evaluation would be an important matter to most teachers because those who did not hold government appointments derived the whole of their incomes from these fees, and even those who did hold such appointments sometimes received fees over and above their salaries (Walden 1909, pp. 326, 178).

The similar practice whereby students paid fees directly to their teachers—greater fees for more esteemed teachers—was a form of student evaluation of instruction that persisted from the early Christian era through the middle ages (Seldin 1980, p. 36) and into the eighteenth century (Werdell 1967). Vestiges of this practice are seen today in some tutorial disciplines (for instance, music) and in voucher plans for educational finance.

Earlier references describe the selection of teachers, but not the evaluation of teachers once selected. In 337 A.D., for example, the appointment of a teacher to headship could be made only after a rhetorical contest. Following the death of Herodes Atticus in 179 A.D., candidates for chairs and professorships were required to demonstrate to a board of electors their familiarity with the tenets of their sect, their philosophical orthodoxy, and some degree of eloquence (Walden 1909, pp. 153, 136). Socrates, of course, was executed in 399 B.C., for having corrupted the youth of Athens by his teachings.

The twentieth-century history of instructional evaluation shows an evolution from some slight interest at the turn of the century to quite intense activity during the 1970s. Morsh and Wilder's exhaustive literature search (1954) lists only a half-dozen studies from 1900 through 1913. Thereafter, the cyclical quality of this history is clear: an increase during the early years of World War I, followed by a decline; another increase in the early 1920s,

3

followed by a decline; a sharp increase for the decade beginning in 1927, then a decline; and a gradual rise beginning shortly after the onset of World War II, peaking in the mid 1970s (during Vietnam); and—the future is not perfectly clear—enduring or tapering off into the 1980s. (See deWolf 1974, for an additional six years of bibliography.)

The mid-1920s, though not a time of especially frequent publication, was nevertheless a significant period in the history of instructional evaluation, for in 1924 a group of Harvard students released the *Confidential Guide to Courses,* probably the first collection of course and instructor evaluations published for use by students in selecting courses. In 1925 the University of Washington began the campuswide collection of student evaluations, with Purdue University and the University of Texas following suit on a more limited scale (Kent 1966, pp. 378, 392; Werdell 1967, p. 3).

Surveys conducted during the 1960s and 1970s illustrate the development of instructional evaluation during that period of vigorous activity. Astin and Lee (1966) report that, of 1,110 deans responding, 96 percent said that classroom teaching was a major factor in evaluating faculty for promotion, salary, and tenure decisions; 80–85 percent said evaluations by deans and chairmen were used in all or most departments; 40–50 percent reported that colleague evaluations and informal student opinion were widely used; and 10–20 percent listed student examination performance, self evaluation, classroom visitation, or systematic student ratings as prominent evaluation methods in their institutions. The high percentage of deans citing dean, chairman, and colleague evaluations, and perhaps informal student opinion, suggests that instructional evaluation was widespread during the 1960s. However, Kent (1966), in a companion article, points out that the low percentages for classroom visitation and systematic student ratings indicate that the evaluations must have been based on hearsay and informal student opinion because neither deans, chairmen, nor colleagues had had the opportunity to observe the classroom instruction. It seems, then, that evaluation practice during the early 1960s was perhaps not so widespread, and surely not so rigorous, as cursory reading of the surveys might have suggested.

Centra (1979, pp. 7–8), comparing the results of his 1977 national survey with those of Astin and Lee, notes that during the intervening decade informal student opinions were largely supplanted by systematic student ratings, which had become as widely used in personnel decisions as colleague opinions. Similarly, he cites data from a 1976 survey indicating that more than half the faculty in more than two-thirds of 734 respondent institutions were using systematic student evaluations in course diagnosis and improvement, substantially more than were using self-, administrator, or colleague evaluations for that purpose. The late 1960s and the 1970s were clearly the period during which systematic student evaluations came into prominence, especially for use in course diagnosis and improvement.

It was also during the 1970s that entire books on instructional evaluation began to appear: Bolton (1973), Miller (1972, 1974), Page (1974), Doyle (1975), and, more recently, Grasha (1977), Centra (1979) and Millman (1981). These books—together with influential monographs by Hildebrand, Wilson, and Dienst (1971) and Ebel (1972); major reviews by Costin, Greenough, and Menges (1971), Trent and Cohen (1973), and Kulik and McKeachie (1975); and conference proceedings edited by Sockloff (1973) and Massey (for example, 1975)—all indicate the evolution of instructional evaluation from fragmented research into a fledgling discipline.

Some rather pronounced changes in the field of instructional evaluation have recently begun to occur. First, as institutional budgets have grown increasingly constrained and as pressures for documentation and substantiation in faculty-personnel decisions have increased, a change in emphasis seems to be taking place from evaluation for instructional improvement to evaluation for promotion, salary, tenure, and even termination decisions. Indeed, in sharp contrast to the posture of previous years, it is no longer rare to hear faculty suggest that the primary purpose of evaluating teaching is making personnel decisions. Second, there seems also to have been a shift from arguing about whether instructional evaluation should be done at all to a concern about how best to use the various kinds of data that are available. The preoccupation with student ratings that was common only a few years ago is slowly being replaced by a more reasonable search for sources of corroboration, especially through peer evaluation. Third, the bipolar attitudes encountered in the recent past, particularly about student evaluations, have softened into widely held feelings of acceptance—or resignation—tinged with healthy skepticism. Finally, the research community has matured into a recognition of the extreme complexity of teaching and the evaluation of teaching; the research methods used to appraise evaluations are becoming very sophisticated, and journal editors are becoming more discriminating.

It is too difficult to resist the temptation to speculate about patterns that seem to emerge in this sketch of the history of instructional evaluation. The acceptance of instructional evaluation does seem directly related to attitudes that value the learner, which are inversely related to authoritarian dispositions. The exceedingly authoritarian methods of the earliest teachers (such as the Sumerians; see Kramer 1963) certainly did not create a climate accepting of evaluation's challenge to the individual authority of teachers; it was not until the Greek emphasis on individual development that the first traces of evaluation appeared. Similarly, the earliest papers in the modern era (for example, Kratz 1896) seem disposed, even biased, toward democratic and humanistic teaching methods. Also, the marked orientation toward personal development that characterized the past fifteen years or so coincides with a dramatic rise in the evaluation of teaching.

Interesting, too, is the juxtaposition of increases in instructional evalua-tion with major social and economic upheavals: the world wars, the war in Vietnam, and the Great Depression. If this is more than sheer coincidence, an explanation may lie with increasing numbers of older, less passive stu-dents (for instance, veterans) enrolling in American colleges and insisting on more control over their education, or in the American penchant for effi-ciency and productivity that seems to manifest itself especially in times of crisis.

In any event, it is clear that evaluation of instruction has been practiced for a very long time, and that interest in evaluation has been especially intense for the past ten or fifteen years. It remains to be seen whether this interest is part of yet another cycle and can be expected to diminish, or whether evaluation has now become institutionalized and future develop-ment will bear more on the flavor than on the essence of evaluation. Very probably, the evolution will depend to a large extent on the ability of evaluation research to keep pace with the increasing sophistication of faculty, administrators, and students, and to a decisive extent on the will of the educational community to maintain the enterprise in the face of the increasingly severe budgetary pressures that clearly lie ahead.

2 Fundamental Issues

The very thought of evaluating teaching raises many difficult issues. Although some of the principal issues are certainly interrelated, and some perhaps identical to one another, it is convenient to discuss them as philosophical issues, psychodynamic issues, and psychometric issues.

Philosophical Issues

Perhaps the most important philosophical issue underlying instructional evaluation arises from a certain tension between the concepts of academic freedom and academic responsibility. The principle of academic freedom gives scholars reign to pursue and share ideas without interference. The principle of academic responsibility requires them to fulfill obligations to the academic community: to research well, to teach well, and to refrain from interfering with other scholars' pursuit and dissemination of knowledge.

Academic freedom is sometimes cited as an argument against evaluating teaching, apparently on the grounds that evaluation often suggests change and change that is not entirely spontaneous is not free. However, a suggestion to change is not necessarily a requirement to change, and, in any event, to extend the principle of academic freedom from the substance to the manner of teaching strains the traditional concept. Moreover, to use the principle of academic freedom as an unqualified reason for not evaluating teaching or, worse, as an excuse for poor teaching, risks doing violence to other people's rights under the principle of academic responsibility.

There may be circumstances, however, under which the academic-freedom argument against evaluating teaching is valid: When evaluation genuinely encumbers the pursuit or dissemination of knowledge. Thus the argument could be valid if, say, anxiety about a peer review or a student survey were to inhibit an instructor from teaching some important course material. Although the inhibition may be more the result of the instructor's anxiety than of the evaluation itself, it is possible for evaluation to be used as a weapon against instructors who teach, for example, politically sensitive courses. In bona fide cases of this sort, the institution needs to assure that

7

the academic freedom of neither teacher, nor students, nor colleagues is violated and that the academic responsibilities of all are fulfilled. This is perhaps best achieved in a deliberative evaluation process, in which the instructor, review-committee members, and administrators can take into account any violations of either principle. Such a process can be augmented by opportunities for the instructor to point out possible violations of these principles, and by effective procedures for redress.

The situation becomes even more difficult in service courses or courses on which subsequent courses depend. Instructors in these courses must balance their freedom to teach what they consider appropriate content against the students' right to receive a widely acceptable grounding in the subject matter, as well as against other instructors' rights to receive well-prepared students. Peer evaluations of course goals and examination content are especially difficult in these courses because of the potential conflict among competing rights. Again the best assurance that academic freedom will be preserved and academic responsibilities fulfilled, in cases such as these, may be the goodwill of the academic community augmented by appropriate and effective legislation.

A second philosophical issue is, do the instructor's credentials, position, and expertise preclude evaluation? One occasionally encounters the argument that, especially in the sanctity of the classroom, there is no authority beyond the instructor, and hence no evaluation of the instructor that could be appropriate. This appears to be the academic-freedom argument intertwined with claims to the ancient prerogatives of royalty and clergy. The position has some validity; witness, for example, the foregoing discussion of the privileges of academic freedom in a peer review, and the inability of students entirely new to a discipline to evaluate the content of a lecture. For the most part, however, this argument fails to persuade. On the contrary one could argue with greater force that teaching must be evaluated, if only to confirm or disconfirm these claims of privilege.

A final philosophical issue reflects academe's inherent cautiousness and perhaps perfectionism or fear of error: Must instructional evaluation await a perfect evaluation technology? Teaching is still imperfectly understood and the instruments of evaluation are in some ways primitive. Faculty, then, trained critics, sometimes direct their considerable critical powers at these deficiencies and propose that "until we know more, we should do nothing." But a glass partially empty is at the same time partially full, so evaluation can proceed if teaching is sufficiently well understood and evaluation technology sufficiently well advanced that teaching can be responsibly albeit imperfectly assessed. Indeed, failure to evaluate may lead to sins more grievous than would evaluation with uncertainty. Instructional and personnel decisions are going to be made in any event, and these decisions are likely to be better the more they are enlightened by responsible evaluation procedures.

Psychodynamic Issues

Most psychodynamic issues in instructional evaluation reduce to the notion of control. Faculty, perhaps more than other people, value doing what they want to do in the way they want to do it. In recent years, however, faculty have been pressed more and more to change their work styles, often by taking on tasks they find distasteful or even threatening and giving up pursuits they hold dear. Moreover, academic performance has suddenly come under greater scrutiny than ever before, and faculty are being required to furnish more and more evidence supporting the amount and quality, and even the value, of what they do. At the same time, they find rewards diminishing—salaries stagnate, grant sources disappear, time for reflection is scarce, appreciation of their effort is rarely expressed. Lurking beneath these external pressures are internal stresses as well. Exceptionally bright people trained in the practice of criticism, they sometimes turn their talents on themselves. Despite the extensive training and the rigorous selection they survived to earn their positions, they can still wonder if, through all of this evaluation, their worst and deepest fears will finally be realized: they will be found out.

Administrators and students are experiencing much the same turmoil. For administrators, every budget cut brings painful decisions; every move is criticized; every decision challenged, even in the courts. Institutions may be becoming ungovernable, and the very attempt at governance is often wearying. For students the cost of education continues to rise, the rewards are in serious doubt, and there is little they can do about it. In short, faculty, administrators, and students often feel they are losing control of their lives.

One effect of this feeling of loss of control is a drive to put things in order. For faculty, this might mean a pressing desire to return to a secure and simpler collegiality without the intrusiveness of evaluation policies and procedures and without such painful responsibilities as the rejection of junior colleagues seeking tenure. For administrators the drive for order might manifest itself in a thirst for objective data to facilitate decisions and remove the burden of subjectivity. For students it might mean a need for confidence in the quality of the education that is offered them and a passion for procedures and mechanisms to guarantee that quality.

The problem is that these drives compete, and efforts to put one group's life in order may further unsettle another's—and there is no ready solution to this conflict of needs. Refining evaluation instruments is desirable, but a simplistic response to deeply held anxieties. Clarifying policies and requirements is useful, but also misses the mark. Providing all the avenues for grievance in the world is still at best a superficial response. Perhaps the most one can do is try to recognize the other people's needs, show a little empathy, improve what can be improved, and press on.

Psychometric Issues

A major psychometric issue in instructional evaluation is, should the evaluation focus on instructional outcomes or on instructional processes. Instructional outcomes are the results of teaching, the diverse aspects of student learning. Process variables are the course and instructor characteristics and instructor behaviors that lead to student learning. Clearly the purpose of teaching is to facilitate learning, and clearly the goal of instructional evaluation is to identify who or what leads to learning. The issue is whether one can approach this goal directly, by measuring learning, or must approach it indirectly, by measuring course and instructor characteristics.

Ideally, one should be able to prepare a really comprehensive final examination, give it to the students, and conclude from the results how good a teacher the course instructor is. Also ideally, one ought to be able to derive from a definitive theory of teaching a list of demonstrably important course and instructor characteristics, measure those characteristics as they obtain in a particular course, and draw a conclusion about the quality of teaching in that course. Each of these approaches, however, has serious problems.

The problems of evaluating teaching by measuring student learning are both philosophical and methodological. Philosophically, it seems unfair to evaluate a person in terms of what other people do or fail to do, at least when those other people are at best only partially under the control of the person being evaluated. Such a practice would be tantamount to attributing to the instructor virtually the total responsibility for student learning. Such a position could also lead to some very odd conclusions, as when students learn (by virtue of their own abilities and motivations) despite a poor instructor, or when they fail to learn (for parallel reasons) from a good one. Methodologically, the technology of testing and statistical analysis is not yet advanced enough for acceptably sure conclusions of these sorts. First, a testing procedure for evaluating teachers would need to account at least for student ability, student knowledge at the beginning of the course, and student motivation throughout the course, so that an instructor does not appear to be good or poor simply because of the capacities of the students in the class. For the same reason, if the test results were to be used to compare one instructor with another, the testing procedure would need to ensure that student differences in ability, motivation, and prior achievement were controlled for by random assignment of students to sections (which is sometimes inconvenient, usually impossible) or by application of statistical adjustments (which do not work so well in practice as they do in theory, see Glass 1974). Second, the tests would need to be identical or at least equivalent in content and difficulty in all courses or sections, so that one instructor did not seem a less effective teacher than another simply because the latter gave an easier test. This kind of arrangement would be relatively easy to accomplish in, say, laboratory sections in beginning chemistry, but exceedingly difficult if one were trying to compare an instructor in Latin grammar to one in Roman history, or an instructor in psychological statistics to one in abnormal psychology. Third, there would need to be some way for instructors to assure themselves (and their colleagues) that the tests did indeed measure the depth and breadth of what their students were supposed to learn, so that people would not be misled into believing that a teacher is effective merely because the students successfully memorized a collection of facts. Finally, there would need to be some central mechanism to make sure that all the necessary controls were in place and to receive and act on appeals.

On the other hand, there is a massive literature that shows that good achievement tests can be derived, and faculty in general do seem to consider even routine classroom tests good enough for use in important decisions about students. Moreover, it is clear that instructors do have some responsibility for whatever learning occurs in their courses. To be reasonable, then, the evaluation plan should take advantage of the strengths of classroom tests without losing sight of their weaknesses.

Evaluating teaching by measuring course and instructor characteristics and behaviors that are indicative of good teaching is certainly no less complex. The principal problem is to determine which characteristics and behaviors to measure. Some seventy years of intense research effort have failed to produce a widely accepted, empirically supported theory or definition of good teaching. Recent research has made matters even more difficult by pointing out the importance of attending to the differential effects of teaching methods on different kinds of students. As unacceptable as it would be to reward or punish instructors on the basis of the dubious results of classroom tests, it would be equally unacceptable to reward or punish them for their conformity to a list of qualities that may have nothing to do with promoting learning in their courses.

But the negative case has again been overstated. Instructional research has made significant progress toward identifying the important features of good teaching, and certain evaluation questionnaire items have been shown to be valid (see chapter 5). As is the case with classroom testing, a reasonable goal would be to devise an evaluation plan that takes advantage of the strengths of process measures, but that also guards against their weaknesses.

Other issues in the application of psychometrics to the evaluation of teaching are: Which sources of information—colleagues, students, or the instructors themselves—can provide acceptable information about which aspects of instruction? What bearing can circumstances surrounding the evaluation have on the information collected? And, how useful and cost effective are evaluation procedures for achieving the various purposes of evaluation? Underlying these issues of psychometric application are issues of psychometric theory: What do *validity* and *reliability* really mean when applied to the instruments, procedures, and data of instructional evaluation? How adequate is traditional psychometrics to the evaluation of evaluation methodology? What advances in psychometric theory seem called for? It is especially at these psychometric issues that the balance of this book is directed.

3 Overview of Instructional Evaluation

There are so many different aspects of instructional evaluation that some kind of structure is helpful to an understanding of the field. Such a structure needs to account for the purposes of evaluation, the sources of evaluative information, the focus of evaluation, the ways that information can be transmitted, and the quality of that information.

Purposes of Evaluation

There are four principal reasons for evaluating teaching: to diagnose and help improve teaching, to aid in administrative decisions regarding individual faculty, to help students choose courses and plan programs, and to provide a criterion for research on teaching itself (Gage 1958, Werdell 1967, Doyle 1975).

Additional reasons are subsumed under these four. Evaluation for diagnosis and improvement can contribute to the improvement not only of the person as a teacher, but also of the teacher as a person; that is, evaluation can assist in personal as well as professional growth. Administrative, or personnel, evaluation can be useful not only in tenure, promotion, and salary decisions but also in the selection of faculty from a pool of applicants, in the placement of faculty according to their particular abilities, and—an unpleasant but, nonetheless, possible application—in the selective termination of faculty in periods of financial exigency. Finally, evaluation for course selection and program planning can mean not only guiding students into courses and curricula suited to their needs and abilities, but also modifying those courses and curricula the better to meet the needs and abilities of the students (Doyle 1975, pp. 3-4).

It is important to distinguish among the reasons for evaluating teaching, because decisions about the sources of information, the focuses on evaluation, and the ways of collecting and transmitting information all flow from the chosen purposes of the evaluation.

Sources of Information

The principal sources of evaluation information are the people who have had the opportunity to observe the processes, materials, or results of teaching: the instructor, current and recent students, and the instructor's colleagues. To these may be added the students' advisors, subsequent teachers, supervisors, and employers; the instructor's supervisors, mentors, and administrative superiors (for example, chairs and deans); specialists in instruction or the evaluation of instruction; alumni, as distinguished from current or very recent students; and anyone else who has had the opportunity to observe some aspect of teaching (for instance, teaching assistants). These people may have observed the processes of teaching directly (in person) or indirectly (for example, through videotapes); or they may have examined the materials or results of teaching (for instance, syllabus, textbooks, examination content; examination performance; enrollment patterns), with or without actual exposure to the instructor.

The essential question regarding the sources of evaluative information is their reliability: which of the sources provides information that is dependable enough to be used? Which of the sources provides the most dependable information?

Focuses of Evaluation

These people—the sources of information—may have looked at any one or more of the many aspects of teaching: the scholarly foundation of the course (that is, the instructor's knowledge of the course material and choice of instructional goals and content); the presentation of the course (the instructor's speaking, discussion-leading, and questioning skills; the instructor's rapport with students; and the instructor's effectiveness at stimulating, motivating, or engaging students); and the effects of the course on the students (attainment of the instructor's—and the student's—intended goals, including achievement and development, attitude change or confirmation, social or vocational or personal growth; as well as serendipitous effects). These aspects of teaching may be considered on any of several levels of abstraction: as specific and discrete behaviors and characteristics (for example, enunciation), molar themes (for example, speaking skills), or summary qualities (general teaching ability, overall student learning).

The essential question about the focuses of evaluation is one of validity: What is good teaching? Or, better, what constitutes good teaching in this particular subject matter for these particular students?

Transmission of Information

Evaluative information can be collected and disseminated in a range of ways. At one extreme is haphazard communication, chance events such as overhearing a few moments of instruction while walking past a classroom door or the accolade or complaint of an occasional student. The probably more reliable ways of giving and receiving information range from fluid to fixed. Fluid methods include, in the evaluation of teaching processes and materials, somewhat structured and systematic conversations or interviews with the instructor, the students, or some other source of information, as well as open-ended or essay-type questionnaire responses; as measures of the results of teaching, fluid methods include oral examinations and essay tests. Fixed methods include checklists, rating scales, and objective tests such as multiple-choice examinations.

The essential questions about these methods have to do with both their reliability and their validity. Are the methods so arranged or constructed that they permit or encourage the communication of whatever dependable information the different sources can provide? Do the conversations, questionnaires, and tests ask the right questions? Do they ask those questions clearly?

Quality of Information

The qualities of information with which psychometrics is principally concerned are validity, reliability, generalizability, and utility. Validity means meaning: What does this item of information signify? What implications, or indirect meaning, does it carry? What information should an evaluation include? Reliability deals with precision: How free is this information from error—mechanical errors of scoring and computing as well as measurement errors ranging from the subtle tendency on the part of raters to mark adjacent items similarly to the gross errors of carelessness and deliberate falsification? Generalizability is representation: Whose opinions and observations does this information represent? How well does this sample of information portray the totality of this instructor's teaching? To what extent do situational factors influence evaluative data? What conditions surrounding the evaluation need to be kept constant—standardized—for the evaluation to be fair? Finally, utility summarizes the situation: What purposes can this information legitimately and cost effectively serve?

Information, from whatever source, about whatever instructional process or result, and gathered in whatever way, needs to be evaluated in terms of each of these four qualities. Thus it is an incomplete practice to scrutinize only student evaluations while assuming that peer evaluations are reliable and valid, or to demand rigorous appraisal of ratings data but not of classroom tests. Only through the simultaneous and parallel assessment of all available kinds of information can an evaluation system be devised that takes advantage of the various strengths and controls for the various weaknesses in the information available for use in the evaluation.

The notion of evaluating evaluative information implies that some purposes for evaluating teaching require information of higher quality than do other purposes. A reasonable ethic in this regard would be that the greater the potential for harm to individuals, the more rigorous the information needs to be. Because neither students nor faculty are likely to be severely and individually harmed by wrong decisions about course presentation and the like, evaluations for course diagnosis and improvement can proceed with information of less rigor than would be required for personnel decisions, in which considerable harm to individual faculty can occur. Similarly, tenure decisions probably require more rigorous information than do salary or promotion decisions, and information used for course selection, because of its public nature, probably needs to be more rigorous than does confidential information for course improvement.

A Conceptual Schema

These five aspects of instructional evaluation—the purposes, focuses, sources, ways of transmitting information, and qualities of information— encompass most of the literature and thinking in the field. Three of these aspects—the focuses, sources, and ways of transmitting information—can be conveniently presented in a conceptual schema that is useful in the study of the field as well as in the devising of instructional evaluation systems. In figure 3-1, the focuses of evaluation are arranged along the vertical axis, the sources of information along the horizontal axis, and the ways of transmitting information along the oblique axis. These three axes outline a cube, the individual cells, and the rows and columns of cells, of which are especially important. The individual cells may be used to raise questions about specific aspects of evaluation: What can information from colleagues, collected by means of conversations, say about the instructor's choice of goals in a course? What can student ratings tell about course presentation? The rows and columns of cells emphasize comparisons: For the evaluation of which focuses is student information appropriate? Which sources of information are acceptable, and which not, in the evaluation of textbook content? Which ways of transmitting information are most congenial and effective for which sources of information? Finally, the purposes of evaluation and the qualities of information can be superimposed on this schema, leading to questions such as: Which sources of information provide the most reliable ratings data about classroom presentation? Which method of transmitting student information is most effective for course-improvement decisions? Which aspects of teaching are validly considered in a peer evaluation for tenure purposes? In the extreme, one could proceed through the entire schema, using a multitude of combinations of axis elements to guide one's study of the field or development of an evaluation plan. More

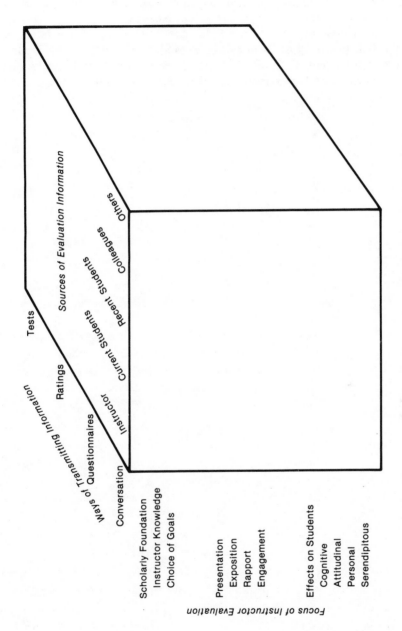

Figure 3-1. Basic Conceptual Schema for Instructional Evaluation

reasonably, one can attend only to the highlights of the schema, the principal focuses, sources, and ways, in an effort to be sure that one's study or one's evaluation plan is comprehensive and balanced.

None of these listings of specific focuses, sources, or ways is intended to be exhaustive. Any of them can be expanded or contracted as circumstances warrant, but the cubic model itself seems to be a useful technique for structuring a rather extensive and detailed body of knowledge.

**Part II:
Focus**

4 Student Learning

The purpose of these focus chapters is to determine which instructional-outcome and instructional-process variables should be emphasized in an evaluation of teaching, that is, to identify those aspects of learning and teaching on which the evaluation should focus. One could think of these chapters as guides to the content of tests and evaluation questionnaires. Later chapters will deal with how best to measure these variables.

Student learning is usually measured by means of tests, but it can also be measured, for instance, by faculty observation of student performance and by students' ratings of their own accomplishment.

Whatever the procedure for measuring learning, an unusually useful aid in defining learning is Bloom's *Taxonomy of Educational Objectives* (1956). Bloom and associates studied huge numbers of specific educational objectives and sorted them into two generally well-articulated hierarchies. In each hierarchy, or taxonomy, the levels of learning are considered progressively more complex, and each successive level is said to subsume those preceding. The first taxonomy covers the cognitive, or intellectual, domain (Bloom et al. 1956); the second the affective, or attitudinal/emotional, domain (Krathwohl, Bloom, and Masia 1964. For a compilation of other attempts to structure educational outcomes, see Lenning 1977.)

Figure 4–1 outlines the cognitive, or intellectual, taxonomy. The main headings in that outline describe the major levels of cognitive learning: The fundamental levels of knowledge, comprehension, and application and the higher levels of analysis, synthesis, and evaluation. *Knowledge* in this context means essentially the remembering of facts. *Comprehension* is one step more involved; it means the beginnings of understanding about the material taught. *Application* refers to the ability to use ideas, methods, or rules in new situations. *Analysis* involves dividing a whole into its elements to understand the interconnections. *Synthesis* is the combining of known elements into a new pattern or structure; and, finally, *evaluation*—the highest level of cognitive activity—entails making judgments about the extent to which something satisfies criteria.

Figure 4–2 summarizes the affective taxonomy. *Receiving* describes the learner's attention or openness to what is being taught. *Responding* signifies a more active attention; it includes becoming interested in the material.

Knowledge
    about isolated pieces of information
    about how to work with these isolated bits
    of information
    about broad patterns of information

Comprehension, or Basic Understanding
    Translating or paraphrasing
    Interpreting or summarizing
    Extrapolating or extending

Application

Analysis
    of pieces, parts or elements
    of interconnections or relationships
    of themes, patterns, or principles

Synthesis
    Construction of a communicable idea
    Construction of a work plan or proposal
    Construction of a paradigm or model

Evaluation
    on the basis of internal standards
    on the basis of external standards

Source: Adapted from Bloom et al. (1956).

Figure 4-1. Taxonomy of Cognitive Outcomes

Valuing means that the learner has come to see worth in the subject, to appreciate it. *Organization* occurs when the learner begins to build a system of values and detemine interrelationships and priorities among the values in that system, and *characterization* means that the learner is behaving in accordance with that system of values, is comfortable with and identified by those values, that, at this highest level, those values have come to comprise the learner's personal philosophy or world view.

For present purposes, the usefulness of these taxonomies is that they can be intersected with an outline of the content of a course to provide a schema for appraising student learning. These schemata are often referred to as "blueprints" or "test plans" (for example, Gronlund 1981, pp. 126–134; Mehrens and Lehmann 1978, pp. 174–180). Figure 4–3 illustrates, on a very general level, a test plan for appraising cognitive learning in an introductory psychology course. Each cell in the plan—the intersection of course topic and level of learning—can be weighted to reflect the importance of

---

Becoming open to information or ideas   **(Receiving)**
    Becoming aware or conscious of . . .
    Becoming willing to notice . . .
    Becoming alert or attentive to . . .

Becoming interested in information or items   **(Responding)**
    Passively, compliantly interested
    Actively, voluntarily interested
    Consenting, pleasurably interested

Coming to value information or ideas   **(Valuing)**
    Accepting, believing in . . .
    Preferring, pursuing . . .
    Adhering or being committed to . . .

Systematizing Values   **(Organization)**
    Relating or connecting values
    Creating a value system

Identification   **(Characterization)**
    Behavioral predisposition, orientation, or set
    Personal identification with a system of values

Source: Adapted from Krathwohl et al. (1964).

Figure 4–2. Taxonomy of Affective Outcomes

that aspect of course content. The weights then determine either the number of test items to be written for each cell or the scoring weights to be assigned to the items. In true/false or multiple-choice tests, for example, there might be at least one item for each cell, more items for more important cells; in essay tests, which necessarily include fewer items, only the most important cells might be represented. Such a test plan is especially useful in helping instructors avoid tests that measure only, say, memorized facts—unless memorization of facts is the only goal in the course.

A parallel procedure could be employed to construct tests or questionnaires that measure affective learning. A test plan thus serves two purposes relevant to the evaluation of teaching. First, it helps the instructor construct tests that are less open to criticism for being too narrow and for not representing the whole of the subject matter. In this respect, the essential step is that the list of topics and list of levels of learning be complete, so that important aspects of cource content are not overlooked. Second, it enables the instructor systematically to write and score test items so the test as a whole mirrors the relative importance of the different parts of the subject matter of the course. Here it is the instructor's judgment of what is impor-

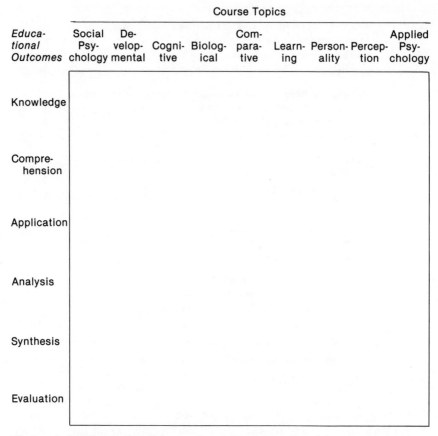

Figure 4-3. Illustrative Schema for Appraising Cognitive Outcomes in a
Beginning Psychology Course

tant that is crucial. Use of a test plan, therefore, makes it more likely that an
evaluation of the test itself will be favorable, and it provides support for the
use of that test as a measure of student learning in evaluating teaching.

Because the typical application of a test plan rests solely on the judgment of the course instructor as to the range and importance of the different
aspects of learning, even the use of tests constructed according to a plan can
still be questionable in the evaluation of teaching. Issues of item difficulty,
student differences, and responsibility for learning aside, to the extent the
instructor's judgment about content importance is sound, the case for using
student learning to evaluate teaching is strengthened; to the extent that that
judgment is deficient, the case is diminished. If student learning is to be
used to evaluate teaching in a particular course, it may be more desirable

to seek a peer review of the test plan before the test is administered (and perhaps forego evaluating test content later) rather than proceed without a review and discover that a review committee has substantial reservation about the content of the test and will therefore not consider the test results.

If student learning is to be used in evaluating teaching, the measures of student learning—tests, questionnaires, or whatever—should be constructed according to a careful plan. The more important the decision to be made on the basis of these measures, the more important it will be that the judgment on which the measures rest is defensible.

5 Instructor and Course Characteristics

To try to list course and instructor characteristics that deserve emphasis in instructional evaluation requires walking a thin line between too much generality and too much specificity. One the one hand, it seems most unlikely that any one set of characteristics will apply with equal force to the teaching of all kinds of material to all kinds of students under all kinds of circumstances. On the other hand, it seems equally unlikely that teaching is entirely idiographic, that there are no principles that apply to a wide range of teaching situations.

To try to prepare such a list also entails substantial risk, because there is as yet no comprehensive and documented theory of teaching from which to draw, and any effort to identify important characteristics in the absence of such a theory necessarily involves considerable inference, if not speculation. Nevertheless, this chapter will attempt to construct a list of course and instructor characteristics that responsible research suggests deserve emphasis in the evaluation of teaching.

Diversity of Teaching

Joyce and Weil's (1972) categorization of teaching models helps underscore the range of instructional activities to which these characteristics must apply and for which underlying principles need to be sought. Joyce and Weil propose four broad families of teaching models. One family consists of those models that emphasize social relationships or group interaction, such as the T-group learning processes of the National Training Laboratory. A second family, which probably corresponds with what most people mean by teaching, stresses information processing, "the ways in which people handle stimuli from the environment, organize data, sense problems, generate concepts and solutions to problems, and employ verbal and non-verbal symbols" (p. 9). Bruner, Piaget, and Ausubel are among the varied theorists whose work focuses on information processing. A third family of models consists of those that deal with the emotions and internal organization of the individual; this orientation is apparent in the work of Rogers, Glasser, Perls, and Hunt. The fourth and final family of teaching models is comprised of those built on the principles of operant conditioning, of which

Skinner's work is the principal example. Joyce and Weil (pp. 11–13) provide a convenient table that summarizes sixteen specific models and classifies them into these four families.

Search for Important Characteristics

Instructor Characteristics

Joyce and Weil identify one principle that is common to all four families of models: teaching under any model requires careful attention to individual differences among students. Cronbach (1967) supports this principle, especially with regard to individual differences in motivation.

Gagné (1970) goes further in the search for principles, however. From his extensive study of the human-learning literature, he proposes twelve conditions for learning that seem to apply to virtually any kind of teaching. Three of these conditions are internal to the student, although they may be indirectly influenced by the teacher; the remaining nine are external to the student and under the direct control of the teacher. The three internal conditions are attentional sets, motivation, and developmental readiness (p. 278). *Attentional sets* are internal processes that enable the learner to select what will be attended to at any particular time. *Motivation* is an internal state that impels the learner to undertake the task of learning, keeps the learner interested in continuing learning, and incites the learner to further learning. *Developmental readiness* is the attainment of a state of intellectual development that enables the learner to accomplish a particular type of learning. Together these three conditions prepare the learner for learning.

Gagné's nine external conditions for learning (1970, p. 304) are self-explanatory: (1) gaining and controlling the learner's attention; (2) informing the learner about intended outcomes; (3) stimulating the learner to recall capabilities already achieved that are prerequisite to the new learning; (4) presenting the learning stimuli; (5) guiding the process of learning; (6) supplying feedback; (7) assessing performance; (8) making provision for transfer of learning to new situations; and (9) taking steps to assure retention. Throughout his writing, Gagné, like Joyce and Weil, stresses the importance of attention to individual differences among students.

Gage and Berliner (1975) searched the literature for teacher behaviors that had been shown to relate to or produce learning. Their study included analysis of major reviews by Rosenshine (1971) and Duncan and Biddle (1974). Although most of the work Gage and Berliner examined had been done on precollege populations, many of the findings seem plausible for older students and have found empirical support in the sparse literature on achievement-producing characteristics of college teachers. As a result of their search, Gage and Berliner focus on four kinds of teacher behavior: structuring, questioning, probing, and rewarding (pp. 691ff). *Structuring* refers to the arrangement of a communication. The most important of the structuring behaviors seems to be signaling, that is, the use of oral statements such as "This is important" or "Now get this" to draw attention to an upcoming point. Ausubel's (1968) theory indicates that these and other organizing statements should provide a framework into which new learning can be embedded (Shulman and Tamir 1973), and Gage and Berliner (pp. 691–692) cite some empirical evidence that signal-giving does contribute to achievement in grade-school and high-school teaching.

Another apparently important aspect of structuring is clarity of exposition, which correlates consistently and substantially with achievement in both precollege and college populations (Gage and Berliner 1975, p. 695; Rosenshine 1971). (Gage and Berliner distinguish clarity from organization. They note that the stronger pattern of association with achievement obtains for clarity, which refers to unambiguous communication. For organization, which pertains to the overall structure of a presentation, their conclusion is that a moderate amount—neither too much organization nor too little—is most efficacious.)

Questioning and probing, or more intense followup questioning, Gage and Berliner conclude, seem to keep students more actively involved in the learning process but show weak and inconsistent relationships with measured learning (pp. 695–701). Questioning and probing, then, as Gagné seems to suggest (1970, p. 278), may be behaviors the usefulness of which is for preparing students to learn.

Rewarding, especially in the form of accepting students' ideas, shows fairly consistent correlations with precollege achievement (Gage and Berliner 1975, pp. 703–711). No parallel studies in the college literature could be located, but operant conditioning principles suggest that rewarding should encourage behavior that precedes it (Skinner 1968; see also the reward features of personal likability, below).

Finally, Gage and Berliner also make the point that at least some of these effects depend on individual differences among students.

Uranowitz and Doyle (1978) concluded from their survey of the social psychology literature that personal likability affects learning in the affective domain, sometimes also in the cognitive domain. In particular, Heider's (1958) balance theory, well supported by empirical research, suggests that people change their beliefs and attitudes to match those of people they like; and Coleman's (1961) reference-group theory, also strongly supported, implies that people who belong to a liked group will change their individual attitudes to conform to those of the group. In the area of precollege cognitive achievement, Uranowitz and Doyle cite a dozen studies that demonstrate that students learn better in the presence of liked persons than in neutral or disliked social surroundings (for example, Lott and Lott 1966, Berkowitz and Zigler 1965, Johnson and Johnson 1975). Among college students, with a more sparse literature based entirely on correlational studies, the results are more mixed. Some studies found no relation between tested learning and students' ratings of their instructor's helpfulness or attitudes toward students (for instance, Doyle and Whitely 1974, Frey 1973). Cohen and Berger (1970), however, found a significant though modest correlation between tested student achievement and rated instructor rapport, and McKeachie, Lin, and Mann (1974; see also McKeachie and Lin 1971) found a significant correlation, especially for women students, between student achievement on a test of higher levels of cognitive operations and student ratings of instructor warmth and rapport. Truax and Carkhuff (1967) cite numerous studies that support the importance of empathy, genuineness, and positive regard in counseling, which has many parallels with teaching (see Curran 1972). Cohen's (1981) meta-evaluation of the literature (see below) on student ratings and student learning found significant positive correlations between achievement and instructor-student rapport in six of twenty-eight studies, nonsignificant positive correlations in seventeen, zero correlations in one study, and nonsignificant negative correlations in four. Uranowitz and Doyle's (1978) conclusion—that these softer qualities are important in affective learning, undemonstrated in cognitive learning among college students—still seems reasonable.

Quite a different avenue to the identification of important course and instructor characteristics is the surveying of students and faculty. Collecting student and faculty opinion about what constitutes good teaching is a weaker research procedure than the experimental and correlational research strategies used in the studies just discussed, because those opinions are vulnerable to problems of stereotyping, social desirability, and perhaps superficiality. Nevertheless, such surveys can add support to other studies and may also suggest potentially important characteristics that deserve more rigorous attention.

Undoubtedly the most extensive of these studies was conducted by Wherry (1952). From university-student essays on effective and ineffective college teaching, Wherry constructed a pool of about 10,000 items, each describing one or more instructor or course characteristics. By eliminating duplicate or too-similar items, he reduced that pool to about 900 items sorted into fifty-two content categories (for example, orientation to student needs, use of motivation technique). Using a variety of statistical procedures designed to identify those characteristics that would most effectively distinguish effective teachers from ineffective ones, including ratings of the importance of each characteristic, he reduced the pool to 300 items, still distributed across the fifty-two content categories. By means of factor analysis, a statistical procedure that, in effect, sorts items on the basis of their empirical interrelationships, he identified twelve themes or factors that underlie the 300 items. He then used this information on underlying themes (factor loadings), along with fourteen other statistical indices, to select a final 140 items representative of all twelve factors. These factors and items describe course and instructor characteristics that Wheery's research indicates deserve attention because students consider them important, because they are unambiguous and ratable, and because they empirically distinguish degrees of instructor effectiveness. Unfortunately, Wherry's factors are not so pure, or unequivocal, as newer statistical procedures would permit, and the content of a fair number of his items are dated.

Doyle (1972) constructed a list of characteristics that included Wherry's final 150 items along with items then in use in student-evaluation programs in nineteen American colleges and universities. He had several hundred undergraduates rate instructors with these items and also rate the importance of each item. By means of statistical procedures similar to but less extensive than Wherry's, Doyle produced a set of sixteen categories of items arranged into four broader families (figure 5–1). As with Wherry's results,

I. Instructor Abilities
   A. Communication: clearly presented the subject matter
   B. Attention: knew how to hold class attention
   C. Cohesiveness: kept the material relevant
   D. Leadership: gained class confidence quickly
   E. Techniques: made good use of examples and illustrations
   F. Control: maintained a classroom atmosphere conducive to learning

II. Instructor Attitudes
   A. Positive Regard: seemed to have a genuine interest in students
   B. Intellectual Openness: was tolerant of other viewpoints
   C. Approachability: was approachable
   D. Nurture: built up confidence in students

III. Encouragement to Intellectual Activity
   A. Intellectual Activation: raised challenging questions
   B. Involvement: was very skillful in directing discussion
   C. Intellectual Expansiveness: related course material to other areas of knowledge
   D. Actualization: was skilled in bringing out the special abilities of students

IV. Effects on Students
   A. Continuation: made you want to study further into the subject
   B. Motivation: knew how to motivate students

Source: Doyle (1972), pp. 222–224. © Kenneth O. Doyle, Jr., Reprinted with permission.

Figure 5–1. Categories of Evaluation Questions, with Illustrative Items

Scale 1. Analytic/Synthetic Approach

1. Discusses points of view other than his own
2. Contrasts implications of various theories
3. Discusses recent developments in the field
4. Presents origins of ideas and concepts
5. Gives references for more interesting and involved points
6. Presents facts and concepts from related fields
7. Emphasizes conceptual understanding

Scale 2. Organization/Clarity

8. Explains clearly
9. Is well prepared
10. Gives lectures that are easy to outline
11. Is careful and precise in answering questions
12. Summarizes major points
13. States objectives for each class session
14. Identifies what he considers important

Scale 3. Instructor-Group Interaction

15. Encourages class discussion
16. Invites students to share their knowledge and experiences
17. Clarifies thinking by identifying reasons for questions
18. Invites criticism of his own ideas
19. Knows if the class is understanding him or not
20. Knows when students are bored or confused
21. Has interest and concern in the quality of his teaching
22. Has students apply concepts to demonstrate understanding

Scale 4. Instructor/Individual Student Interaction

23. Has a genuine interest in students
24. Is friendly toward students
25. Relates to students as individuals
26. Recognizes and greets students out of class
27. Is accessible to students out of class
28. Is valued for advice not directly related to the course
29. Respects students as persons

Scale 5. Dynamism/Enthusiasm

30. Is a dynamic and energetic person
31. Has an interesting style of presentation
32. Seems to enjoy teaching
33. Is enthusiastic about his subject
34. Seems to have self-confidence
35. Varies the speed and tone of his voice
36. Has a sense of humor

Source: Hildebrand, Wilson, and Dienst (1971), pp. 18–19. Reproduced with permission.
Note: Based on 1968 survey. N = 1015.

Figure 5-2. Components of Effective Teaching as Perceived by Students

Scale 1. Research Activity and Recognition
1. Does work that receives serious attention from others
2. Corresponds with others about his research
3. Does original and creative work
4. Expresses interest in the research of his colleagues
5. Gives many papers at conferences
6. Keeps current with developments in his field
7. Has done work to which I refer in teaching
8. Has talked with me about his research

Scale 2. Intellectual Breadth
9. Seems well read beyond the subject he teaches
10. Is sought by others for advice on research
11. Can suggest reading in any area of his general field
12. Knows about developments in fields other than his own
13. Is sought by colleagues for advice on academic matters

Scale 3. Participation in the Academic Community
14. Encourages students to talk with him on matters of concern
15. Is involved in campus activities that affect students
16. Attends many lectures and other events on campus
17. Has a congenial relationship with colleagues

Scale 4. Relations with Students
18. Meets with students informally out of class
19. Is conscientious about keeping appointments with students
20. Meets with students out of regular office hours
21. Encourages students to talk with him on matters of concern
22. Recognizes and greets students out of class

Scale 5. Concern for Teaching
23. Seeks advice from others about the courses he teaches
24. Discusses teaching in general with colleagues
25. Does not seek close friendships with colleagues (Negative)
26. Is someone with whom I have discussed my teaching
27. Is interested in and informed about the work of colleagues
28. Expresses interest and concern about the quality of his teaching

Source: Hildebrand, Wilson, and Dienst (1971), pp. 21–22. Reproduced with permission.
Note: Based on 1967 survey. N = 119

Figure 5–3. Components of Effective Teaching as Perceived by Colleagues

Doyle's items described characteristics that students considered important, that were ratable, and that distinguished levels of instructor effectiveness.

Hildebrand, Wilson, and Dienst (1971) asked faculty as well as students to identify important course and instructor characteristics. Figures 5-2 and 5-3 present the faculty list and the student list. The lists seem similar with respect to characteristics that could be observed outside the classroom (that is, broadly knowledgeable, genuinely interested in students), different with respect to characteristics that especially reflect the vantage points of the two groups (that is, clarity and enthusiasm in teaching versus research productivity). Both lists also include characteristics that have to do with intellectual breadth and relationships with students.

More than three dozen studies have examined the relationship between student learning and characteristics such as those produced by Wherry, Doyle, and Hildebrand, Wilson, and Dienst. Cohen (1981) employed meta-analytic techniques (Glass 1976) to synthesize this body of research. He located forty-one separate studies covering sixty-eight multisection courses in a wide variety of disciplines, although the courses were offered almost exclusively on the introductory level. Table 5-1 shows the average correlation between tested student learning and each of seven categories of instructor or course characteristics, along with the range of correlation that, given measurement error, is very likely to include the true correlation, and a tabulation of the number of significant and nonsignificant positive and negative correlations in each study. In addition, table 5-1 presents the same statistics for student progress (that is, students' self-ratings of accomplishment) and for two summary rating items: overall course effectiveness and overall teaching ability. Cohen's results support the importance of characteristics that have to do with overall teaching ability, instructor skill, structure, and, to a lesser extent, rapport, self-rated student accomplishment, and overall course effectiveness. Cohen's analysis also showed that these correlations were higher when the instructors were regular faculty rather than graduate students, when the students knew their grades before the evaluation, and when the classroom exams were scored by someone other than the course instructor.

Cohen's analysis did not distinguish among the various specific instructor skills grouped under the general-skill category. However, studies by Frey (1973), Sullivan and Skanes (1974), and Doyle and Whitely (1974) found quite consistent positive correlations between tested student learning and instructor clarity of presentation and ability to motivate students.

This diverse literature—the careful analyses of experimental and correlation studies provided by Gagné (1970) and Gage and Berliner (1975), the systematic opinion surveys by Wherry (1952), Doyle (1972), and Hildebrand, Wilson, and Dienst (1971), and the meta-analysis by Cohen (1981)—provides the foundation for a list of course and instructor characteristics that deserve emphasis in the evaluation of teaching. Figure 5-4 presents such a list. This list could easily be turned into a questionnaire for student, peer, or self-evaluation of teaching. A few of the items in figure 5-4 are already in common use on evaluation questionnaires, but many of them are untried and therefore need to be screened, at least to be sure that the raters

Table 5-1
Results of a Meta-Analysis of Student-Evaluation Validity Studies

Rating Dimension[1]	N	Mean Correlation	95% Confidence Interval	Positive SIG	Positive NS	Zero	Negative SIG	Negative NS
		Mean Rating/Achievement Correlational Effect Sizes[1]		Significant and Nonsignificant, Positive, Zero, and Negative Correlations[2]				
Overall Course	22	0.47	0.09, 0.73	11	9	0	0	2
Overall Instructor	67	0.43	0.21, 0.61	30	29	0	1	7
Skill	40	0.50	0.23, 0.70	20	17	0	0	3
Rapport	28	0.31	−0.07, 0.61	6	17	1	0	4
Structure	27	0.47	0.11, 0.72	9	15	0	0	3
Difficulty	24	−0.02	−0.42, 0.39	0	12	2	1	9
Interaction	14	0.22	−0.36, 0.67	4	8	1	0	1
Feedback	5	0.31	−0.79, 0.94	1	4	0	0	0
Evaluation	25	0.23	−0.18, 0.58	4	16	2	0	3
Student Progress	14	0.47	−0.08, 0.80	4	6	2	0	2

Sources: 1. Peter Cohen. "Student Ratings of Instruction and Student Achievement: A Meta-Analysis of Multisection Validity Studies." *AERJ*, 1981, 51 (3), pp. 281–309. Copyright 1981, American Educational Research Association, Washington, D.C.
        2. Compiled from Cohen (1981), pp. 294–298.

Helps students distinguish what is important from what is not
Helps students stay interested in learning
Tailors the presentation to the student's level of development
Tries to reach all the different kinds of students in the course
Works to keep students attentive
Keeps students aware of the course goals
Helps students bring prior learning to bear on new material
Presents the subject matter clearly
Provides the right amount of structure: neither too much nor too little
Guides students in their study
Provides helpful feedback
Helps students apply what they have learned to new situations
Helps students keep hold of what they have learned
Is approachable
Respects students
Understands students
Keeps students challenged
Knows the subject well enough
Emphasizes what is important in the field

Figure 5–4. Proposed List of Important Instructor Characteristics

understand what they mean and can answer them. That is, these items still need to be assessed for reliability. The advantage of these items is that, in comparison to most sets of questionnaire items, they are more closely tied to research literature on student learning, and therefore may constitute a more valid measure of effective college teaching.

The items in figure 5–4 represent rather specific characteristics. Doyle (1975; see also Doyle 1979, and Scriven 1981), however, recommended the use of general, summary items, especially in personnel evaluation, because it is very difficult to argue that these summary items are not applicable to any given course, and because these items have been shown to be more related to student learning than are most specific items. Three summary items are in common use in student questionnaires:

How would you rate this instructor's overall teaching ability?

How would you rate the overall effectiveness of this course?

How much have you learned as a result of this course?

The first of these items summarizes specific instructor characteristics, the second summarizes course characteristics, and the third summarizes student learning. Cohen's meta-analysis (table 5–1) confirms that items such as these relate consistently to empirically tested student learning. Such items are indeed among the best indirect measures of effective learning.

Characteristics of Reading Materials and Tests

The characteristics examined thus far have dealt principally with the course instructor, but there are at least two other important course components that need to be addressed, reading materials and tests.

Textbooks and other reading materials may be the single most neglected component of instruction—though they may often be the most important. Textbooks have obvious advantages and disadvantages compared to actual teachers. Textbooks can be reread, paused over, marked up; for communication of information they may be the most effective medium available. On the other hand, textbooks cannot readily vary their presentation to meet the needs of different students, nor do they often maintain a real dialogue with students. Textbooks are probably much less effective than good teachers in helping students achieve higher-order course objectives.

A list of the important qualities of textbooks and other reading materials is probably not very different from the list of important characteristics of teachers furnished in figure 5–4. A good textbook, for example, should certainly keep students' attention, inform students about intended outcomes, structure its presentation clearly, indicate which material is especially important, and motivate students to stay involved in the course. Indeed, there are few qualities in figure 5–4 that do not seem important in the evaluation of reading materials. It is surprising, therefore, that so little research has apparently been done on the role of reading materials in facilitating learning. In the absence of such research, figure 5–4 may furnish a tentative outline of the important qualities of reading materials.

The evaluation of tests, examinations, and other direct measures of student learning is a discipline in itself (see, for example, Thorndike 1971). A classroom test is most properly evaluated by examining the extent to which its content reflects the goals of the course and by statistical item-analysis procedures. Other qualities of a test, such as its fairness or 'pickiness', are subordinate to those principal qualities. A test's mirroring of the important content of the course—its content validity—is evaluated by the kinds of test-plan procedures described in chapter 4. Item-analysis strategies depend on whether the test is norm referenced or criterion referenced.

Norm-referenced tests are those for which a score is intepreted in relation to the other scores. A classroom test "graded on the curve" is thus norm-referenced. Criterion-referenced, or mastery, tests are those for which a score is interpreted relative to some preestablished standard of minimum competency, such as a passing score of 80. Driver's licensing tests are often criterion referenced. Most classroom tests are norm referenced; their purpose is to differentiate among students for purposes of assigning grades.

Item analysis for norm-referenced tests focuses on the difficulty of the test (as well as the difficulty of each separate item) and on t' ɔ test's (as well as each item's) ability to distinguish levels of student performance, its discriminating power. A good norm-referenced test is neither too difficult nor too easy for the majority of people who take it. More precisely, the best norm-referenced tests for typical classroom use are composed of items of middle difficulty, such that about half the students get the typical item right and half get it wrong. Test difficulty and discriminating power are closely related. Tests that are too easy or too hard will not differentiate among levels of student performance so well as will tests that contain a preponderance of middle-difficulty items. Therefore an easy way to evaluate the difficulty and estimate the discriminating power of a test is simply to compute, for each item, the percentage of students who answer correctly. If those percentages cluster around 60 percent–75 percent[1], the test is of proper difficulty and is most likely adequately discriminating. More easily still, although this provides less information, one could simply compute the ratio of the average score on the test to the highest possible score. If that ratio is in the 60–75 percent range, the test is probably, in item-analysis terms, a good one.

Although items of proper difficulty will tend also to be discriminating, a direct appraisal of discriminating power is always desirable. Because discrimination is merely the degree to which a test item distinguishes students who do well on the whole test from students who do poorly, a straightforward procedure for estimating item discrimination is to select, on the basis of total test score, the top and bottom 25 percent or so of students in the class and, for each item, subtract the number of students in the bottom group who got the item right from the number in the top group who got it right, dividing that difference by the number of students in the top (or bottom) group. This procedure will produce a coefficient that can vary from −1.00 to +1.00. This discrimination coefficient should always be positive, otherwise the poorer students are getting the item right.

Finally, for the sake of completeness, one should look at the number of students who chose the various incorrect responses. Ideally, approximately equal numbers of student should have chosen each incorrect alternative. If one particular incorrect alternative attracted a disproportionate share of students, there is either a common misunderstanding in the class or that alternative was misleading and ought to be rewritten.

Item analysis for criterion-referenced tests is very different from that for norm-referenced tests because criterion-referenced tests are not intended to differentiate among students. Hence, neither difficulty nor discriminating power is relevant. Procedures for item analysis of criterion-referenced tests are not yet well developed, but a reasonable statistic is Krypsin and Feldhusen's Index of Sensitivity to Instructional Effects, described in Gronland (1981, p. 266).

Item-analysis procedures for essay tests are parallel to those for objective tests, with the complication that scores on essay tests are influenced by some degree of unreliability in scoring. The test-scoring offices of many colleges and universities provide inexpensive and convenient item-analysis services.

To summarize, the focus of the evaluation of typical norm-referenced classroom tests should be the content and the difficulty and discriminating power of those tests as determined by statistical analysis. The focus of the evaluation of reading materials should probably be those qualities that parallel the qualities of effective teachers, and the focus of the evaluation of college teachers, at least insofar as indirect, process evaluation is concerned, should probably be a list of research-supported characteristics such as those in figure 5-4, along with summary characteristics as overall teaching ability, overall course effectiveness, and overall student learning.

First Search for Interactions

These characteristics, however, may not be absolutes; that is, some characteristics may be more important in helping students achieve some kinds of learning, while other characteristics may be more important for other kinds. Moreover, some characteristics may be more important in some of Joyce and Weil's (1972) families of teaching models, while other characteristics play a greater role in other models. These interrelationships constitute what researchers call interactions.

Although there is relatively little really persuasive empirical evidence so far that interactions of these sorts are dependable enough or strong enough to influence evaluations of teaching (Cronbach and Snow 1977), the notion of interactions is so inherently attractive that it deserves consideration. Figure 5-5 draws together the list of instructor characteristics developed in this chapter, the list of cognitive and affective outcomes outlined in chapter 4, and the four families of teaching models provided by Joyce and Weil (1972). Each cell in the cube represents one combination of instructor characteristic, student outcome, and teaching method. Interactions exist to the extent that the importance of an instructor characteristic varies across either outcomes or teaching methods, or an outcome is more influenced by different characteristics or methods, or a method is more compatible with some outcomes or instructor characteristics than with others.

An instructor's ability to build on student differences in motivation is

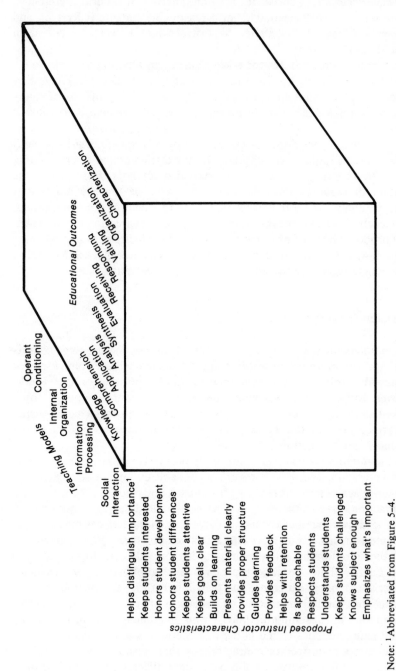

Note: [1] Abbreviated from Figure 5–4.

Figure 5–5. Schema for Guiding a Search for Instructor × Outcome × Teaching-Model Interactions

probably important in each of the four families of teaching methods. The most probable interactions seem to be for rapport and acceptance of students' ideas, which may be less important in operant conditioning methods and information processing, and clarity of presentation, which may be less important in teaching methods that deal with social learning and emotions. Similarly, building on motivational differences is probably important for each kind of outcome, but clarity characteristics may bear more on cognitive outcomes, while rapport characteristics may be more associated with affective outcomes. This pattern appears to continue insofar as information-processing methods seem more germane to the cognitive outcomes, and social and emotive methods to affective outcomes; but conditioning methods are probably applicable to any outcome. Thus it seems not surprising that one might want to focus more on the Gagné characteristics when the goal of teaching is cognitive achievement, and on the rapport characteristics when the goal is affective learning. Further research would be necessary to confirm this hypothesis.

Final Qualities: Knowledge and Black Marks

Conspicuous by its absence so far has been any mention of an instructor's grasp of the course material as an important focus in evaluation. Degrees, rank, and other credentials suggest subject-matter competence, but these suggestions may not always be dependable. Graduate assistants new to the field or regular faculty teaching courses outside their areas of demonstrated expertise may not always have a firm grasp of the course material. Moreover, even regular faculty may not always be current in all fields in which they teach, and many would probably admit that there are topics within their usual courses with which they are not entirely comfortable.

Assessment of an instructor's grasp of the subject matter of each course he or she teaches should therefore also be a focus of evaluation. This appraisal should probably be along the lines of a peer review of scholarship, with attention not only to prior training but also to current activities that seem to enhance knowledge. Although introspection suggests that one teaches more fluently to the extent of one's grasp of the subject (see also Verderber 1976, on extemporaneous speaking), the possibility that too much instructor knowledge may be as counterproductive as too little (Elliott 1950) deserves to be explored. That is, an instructor may need only a sufficient grasp of the subject matter to teach effectively (Doyle 1975, p. 68).

The last focus of evaluation consists of what Scriven (1981 and personal communication) has described as "black marks." Black marks refer to behaviors or traits that would not typically enter into a theory of teaching but that nevertheless may be very important in evaluation: genuinely racist

or sexist postures, for example, or other violations of academic responsibility such as unsatisfactorily explained absence from class or chronic tardi-
ness. Scriven suggests appending a checklist of black-mark categories to a
student evaluation form, the results to be attended to only if significant
numbers of students respond affirmatively. In whatever appropriate way
such information is collected, it can legitimately be considered in an evaluation on grounds either of institutional policy or academic responsibility.

Note

1. Because of the effects of guessing, middle difficulty varies with the
form of test item. For true/false items, middle difficulty is 75 percent; for
four-alternative multiple-choice items, 62.5 percent; for five-alternative
items, 60 percent. Middle difficulty is the point midway between the highest
possible score and the score that could be achieved by sheer guessing.

6 Student Characteristics

The reason for looking at student characteristics in an evaluation of teaching is qualitatively different from the reason for looking at course and instructor characteristics and learning outcomes. Learning outcomes and course and instructor characteristics are variables the measurement of which is in itself evaluative; the measurement of student characteristics is not itself evaluative but helps in the interpretation of more properly evaluative measures by permitting the appraisal of additional interactions, for example, the extent to which an instructor is more effective with some kinds of students than with others.

Students vary on many dimensions. For example, deWolf (1974) lists seventy-six student characteristics, from age to amount of travel experience, that have been studied in relation to student ratings. In the search for important student characteristics, as in the search for instructor and course characteristics, one needs to be satisfied with the goal of identifying qualities that *very often* are important, recognizing that in specific circumstances even the most unusual variable might be important and that there may be no variables that are *always* important.

Student characteristics seem to fall into three broad classes: biographical variables as age and sex, ability variables, and personality variables, including motivation and cognitive style.

Biographical Characteristics

Although no formal meta-analysis of biographical characteristics could be located, a perusal of studies of student sex and year in school (see Morsh and Wilder 1954) suggests that as a rule these characteristics are unrelated to students' evaluation of their teachers (Doyle 1975, pp. 73–74). Moreover, when relationships between student biographics and student evaluations are found, they are usually of such small magnitude that their influence is trivial in the overall picture (for example, Doyle and Whitely 1974).

There do seem to be two exceptions to this rule, however, one empirical and quite general, the other logical and rather specific. Costin, Greenough, and Menges (1971) and Doyle (1972, p. 33) cite a number of studies that suggest that more advanced students—upper-division students, graduate students—tend to give more favorable ratings than do less advanced students, perhaps because the more advanced students have grown wise enough at last to recognize good instruction, or because they have become desensitized to poor instruction, or simply because they have different needs than do their younger cohorts, needs more frequently satisfied by typical instructors. Empirically, then, year in school seems to be an important student characteristic.

The logical exception to the rule that student biographics can generally be disregarded is that in particular circumstances there can and probably should be a relationship between student satisfaction or achievement and almost any student biographical variable. In a course on modern sex roles taught to male and female students from a strongly feminist (or anti-feminist) point of view, one should expect to find a correlation between student sex and student evaluations; or in a course in which the instructor consistently attends to the needs of majors at the expense of nonmajors, there ought to be a relationship between student ratings and major field. Thus, in specific circumstances, almost any student characteristic can be important.

Ability Characteristics

Student ability is usually measured by tests such as the Scholastic Aptitude Test or by course grades. Some studies have found no relationship between ability measures and student evaluations, others have found significant relationships, usually positive but sometimes negative (Doyle 1975, p. 74). This apparent inconsistency was well explained by Remmers, Martin, and Elliott (1949): Facing a class composed of students of varying ability, an instructor can gear the course to the quicker, the average, or the slower students. That choice will determine the relationship between the ability and ratings. For example, if the instructor gears the teaching to the quicker students, these students should be relatively more satisfied and the correlation will be positive. If the course is more directed at the slower students, these students will be more satisfied—and the quicker ones less so—and the correlation will be negative. Elliott (1950) provides data that substantiate this explanation. Thus student ability may also be an important characteristic in the interpretation of evaluations. Feldman's thoughtful analysis (1977) notes that, in addition to student ability, the students' actual grades in the course *in comparison to* their usual grades may also relate to the evaluations they give.

Personality Characteristics

Recent literature suggests modest but dependable relationships among certain personality variables, teaching methods, and student satisfaction and achievement. McKeachie (1978, pp. 248–250), for example, concludes from a brief literature review that more flexible students seem more satisfied and productive when teachers give them opportunity for self-direction, while authoritarian students prefer more controlled and structured approaches to teaching. Domino (1971) found significant relationships between students' ratings of overall teacher effectiveness and student achievement orientation as measured by the achievement-via-independence and achievement-via-conformity scales of the California Psychological Inventory. Domino, too, found significant interactions: Conforming students taught "in a conforming manner" and independent students taught "in an independent manner" gave more favorable ratings and learned more than did students taught in a manner not consonent with their achievement orientation. Authoritarianism/flexibility and conformance/independence seem to have in common an element of need for control which may be another important student characteristic.

The centrality of motivational factors to the instructional process has already been noted with regard to teacher characteristics. Motivation is no less important as a student characteristic (Gagné 1970, p. 282). Moen (1978) proposed a three-dimensional model of academic motivation, from which Moen and Doyle (1977) and Doyle and Moen (1978) empirically derived a set of sixteen motivations that could be measured with adequate reliability (figure 6–1). Among these, three clusters are especially interesting because they seem to coincide with three dimensions that underlie most personality inventories (Tellegen 1976) and because they may be useful in defining student types. The thinking, persisting, and achieving motives together comprise a dimension that might be called positive orientation toward school. Students who enjoy the cognitive processes in school work, who tend to persist at a task, and who want to do their best can be said to have a positive orientation toward school. The withdrawing motives and the dislike-school and discouraged-about-school scales form a cluster that describes a negative orientation toward school. Loners who lack interest and find schoolwork futile thus are considered to have a negative orientation. Finally, the influencing and competing motivations, along with facilitating anxiety, form a potency cluster comprising high-energy, hard-driving, high-potency students who thrive under pressure, in contrast to low-potency students who avoid discussions, endure confrontation, and crumble under pressure.

Moen's analysis brings to mind the social-perceptions schema developed by Wilson Learning Corporation, Minneapolis, for use in interpersonal and sales training. According to this schema, people can be classified as "drivers," "expressives," "amiables," and "analytics", and any given pairing of these types will result in specified outcomes. Wilson Learning Corporation researchers have devised lists of suggestions for facilitating relationships with people of each type. This work is in many ways parallel to instructional evaluation and merits the attention of independent researchers.

Thinking Motives. Enjoying the cognitive processes of schoolwork; e.g., thinking, analyzing, synthesizing.

Persisting Motives. Tending to keep working at something until it is completed.

Achieving Motives. Desiring to work hard and do one's best.

Facilitating Anxiety. Pressure or anxiety is enjoyable and/or helps the person do better work.

Debilitating Anxiety. Pressure, anxiety, or the possibility of failure are painful and interfere with doing good work.

Grades Orientation. Desiring good grades.

Economic Orientation. Focusing on the career preparation aspect of school.

Desire for Self-Improvement. Emphasizing improvement of self-understanding, knowledge, and general competence through school.

Demanding. Refusing to passively accept disliked teaching practices.

Influencing Motives. Enjoying arguing with others or being a leader.

Competing Motives. Desiring to do better than others.

Approval Motives. Identifying the desire for praise or acceptance as an explicit reason for trying to learn or do well in school.

Affiliating Motives. Enjoying being with other people in school.

Withdrawing Motives. Preferring to work alone; finding group projects or class discussions unprofitable or unpleasant.

Dislike School. Disliking school, lacking interest, preferring other activities.

Discouraged about School. Feeling that school is too hard or that it does little good to study.

Source: © Ross E. Moen and Kenneth O. Doyle, Jr. Reprinted with permission.

Figure 6–1. Sixteen Measurable Academic Motivations

Subsequent research (Moen, personal communication) has shown that students with a positive orientation toward school tend to give more favorable ratings to their instructors on many evaluation items, and that students with a negative orientation tend to give generally unfavorable ratings. High-potency students may give either favorable or unfavorable ratings depending on the circumstances: favorable ratings when the kind of teaching they encounter allows or encourages them to unleash their energy in interpersonally challenging situations, unfavorable ratings when it does not. In contrast, low-potency students give favorable ratings in situations that respect their discomfort, unfavorable ratings when the circumstances are threatening. Moen's research has also confirmed McKeachie's (1978, p. 248) conclusion that students high in affiliating motivation should tend to give more favorable evaluations in interpersonally supportive and noncompetitive situations.

In short, knowing the motivational groups to which students belong, especially in relation to the kind of teaching they encounter, may add further meaning to their ratings. Hence these motivational characteristics are also important in the evaluation of teaching.

Messick (1970) and Witkin (1976) have strongly recommended study of the interaction of student evaluations and cognitive styles, or modes of thinking and learning. Initial studies using traditional measures of cognitive style (Crockett 1975, Witkin 1976, Wright and Richardson 1977, and Packer and Bain 1978) have reported some significant interactions between these styles and students' perceptions of teaching. Because the traditional measures are generally too cumbersome for routine use in instructional evaluation, Trabin and Doyle (1981; see also Church, Trabin, and Doyle 1981) attempted to write questionnaire items that would serve as convenient measures of major cognitive styles. The styles they selected were cognitive complexity and integrative complexity. Cognitive complexity (Kelly 1955, Bieri et al. 1966) is defined as the capacity to construe social behavior multi-dimensionally; the special characteristic of cognitively complex people is their ability to differentiate others in terms of roles and attributes. Integrative complexity (Harvey, Hunt, and Schroeder 1961) is a style—better, perhaps, a sequence of styles—that evolves from concrete to increasingly abstract capabilities for viewing the world. Integratively simple people— "dualists" (Perry 1968)—see things as black or white, right or wrong, good or bad; they deal in absolutes. People who are more integratively complex—for example, Perry's "relativists"—see a diversity of alternatives they evaluate for comparative strengths and weaknesses before making a commitment. Integratively complex people deal in shades of gray.

Trabin and Doyle's first questionnaire item was fashioned after Bloom's (1956) hierarchy of cognitive operations, their second item after Perry's (1968) theory of cognitive development. Their third item was an attempt to measure the essence of these styles in terms of structured versus unstructured teaching strategies. The three items appear as items 7, 8, and 9 in figure 6-2.

These items all provided reliable measurement of student differences along a continuum of concreteness to abstractness. They were statistically significant (though not very powerful) predictors of variability in student ratings: more abstract or complex students tended more to differentiate among rating items, while more concrete or cognitively simple students tended to give more similar ratings on the various items. These questionnaire items were modestly related to the overall level of student evaluations in that the more abstract students tended to give less favorable evaluations in these courses. However, efforts to identify interactions between student and instructor cognitive styles, such that, for example, more complex students preferred more complex instructors, were unsuccessful. Trabin and Doyle (1981) and Church, Trabin, and Doyle (1981) concluded that this avenue of research seemed promising but that their questionnaire items were only partially successful as convenient and inexpensive measures of cognitive style.

Witkin's (1976) and Packer and Bain's (1978) work on field depen-dence/independence and Wright and Richardson's (1977), Trabin and Doyle's (1981) and Church, Trabin, and Doyle's (1981) work on complexity suggest that these styles are potentially important factors in the interpre-tation of instructional evaluations, but that more attention needs to be given to the practical measurement of these characteristics.

So, this search for student characteristics that can often help in the interpretation of instructional evaluations by indicating the extent to which an instructor is more effective with some kinds of students than with others has come up with a list that includes year in school, academic ability, need for control, several aspects of academic motivation, and, tentatively, several aspects of cognitive style. Figure 6-2 presents a list of questionnaire items that might measure these characteristics. Figure 6-3 (page 50) casts these characteristics in yet another cubic schema to recall the likelihood of interactions involving student characteristics, instructor and course characteristics, and student outcomes.

---

1. In which year in school are you?
   Freshman   Sophomore   Junior   Senior   Graduate

2. Which of the following best describes your typical grades?
   _____   Almost all A's
   _____   Mostly A's and B's
   _____   Mostly B's and C's
   _____   Mostly C's or lower

3. What grade do you expect to receive in this course?
   Higher than I   About the same as I   Lower than I
   usually get   usually get   usually get

Source: © University of Minnesota Measurement Services Center. Reproduced with permission.

Figure 6-2. Experimental Questions that Might Measure Some Important
                Student Characteristics

Figure 6-2 continued

4. How do you feel when things seem to be getting out of control in your life?
    Very Uncomfortable   Uncomfortable   Comfortable   Very Comfortable

5. How would you summarize your overall feelings toward school?
    Very Negative   Negative   Positive   Very Positive

6. Please rank the following statements as to how well they describe you:
    (1 = Best description, 2 = Next Best, etc.)
    _____ I enjoy school; I'm persistent and want to do my best.
    _____ I find school boring, futile; I prefer to be by myself.
    _____ I'm very energetic, a "driver"; I enjoy pressure.
    _____ I hate pressure; I try to avoid confrontations.

7. I learn best when the task is to:
    (Please rank these answers from 1-5 with 1 = best, 2 = next best, etc.)
    _____ show an idea can be applied to an actual situation.
    _____ master a set of concrete facts or a body of information.
    _____ closely examine abstract ideas and theories.
    _____ understand basic principles about a subject.
    _____ put together several differing ideas into a theory that makes sense
            to me.

8. I learn best when the task is to:
    (Please rank these answers from 1-3 with 1 = best, 2 = next best, etc.)
    _____ take a position after considering many ways of interpreting a
            difficult problem.
    _____ figure out the one right answer to a straightforward problem.
    _____ choose the best answer from many possible ones which seem
            equally good.

9. I learn best when:
    (circle one answer)
    a. the teacher provides the information and I figure out the main
        connecting themes on my own.
    b. the teacher explains the major themes and I study the information
        on my own.

10. To what extent did you feel "on the same wave length" with your
    instructor?

Very Little	Little	Some	Much	Very Much	Extremely Much
1	2	3	4	5	6

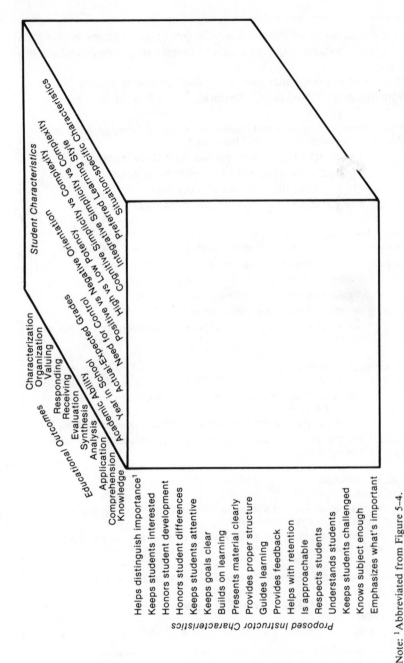

Note: [1] Abbreviated from Figure 5-4.

Figure 6–3. Schema for Guiding a Search for Student × Instructor × Outcome Interactions

7 Issues in the Validation of Evaluations

The principal concern in the development of methods for evaluating teaching is that the methods be valid, that is, that they focus on matters that bear somehow on student learning. Accordingly, chapter 4 described a procedure for determining which aspects of learning ought to be examined; chapter 5 proposed a set of instructor and course characteristics that seem important to learning; and chapter 6 enumerated important characteristics of the learners themselves. Together these chapters provide a focus for evaluation. The purpose of this chapter is to address some of the technical issues underlying the validity of methods for evaluating teaching.

Validity means meaning. Thus validation is the process of attributing meaning to data. The many procedures that may be used in the validation of an evaluation method are usually classified under the headings of content validation, criterion-oriented validation, and construct validation (American Psychological Association 1966). *Content validation* means the attribution of meaning through expert judgment about the importance of the questions to be asked. The goal of content validation is to produce a set of questions each of which qualified judges consider important that together cover the full range of important points. The judgment of the course instructor provides a degree of content validity for a final examination, although the judgment of a panel of qualified faculty might constitute stronger evidence. Surveys of students and faculty for their opinions about which instructor and course characteristics are important provide some content validity for evaluation questionnaires (for example, see Wherry 1952, Doyle 1972, Hildebrand, Wilson, and Dienst 1971). Content validity rests on the quality of judgments, hence on the qualifications of the judges.

Criterion-oriented validity assigns meaning by relating the measure at hand—for instance, a proposed evaluation question—to some separate measure of known validity. Thus a proposed college-admissions test is considered valid to the extent that it correlates with some suitable criterion measure such as grade-point average. Similarly, studies that examine the correlations between evaluation ratings and student achievement are considered to be criterion-oriented validity studies.

Construct validation is qualitatively different from content and criterion-oriented validation. In fact, it subsumes both of them. Construct validation—the attribution of meaning to a hypothetical construct—is a philosophy-of-science procedure that attributes meaning through a process of repeated hypothesis-generation and testing, through a process of theory building. The goal of construct validation is to develop a hypothetical construct by successive refinements of a measure of that construct. The process of refining that measure requires the weaving of a network of hypotheses and empirical findings around the proposed construct through the use of content-validation procedures, criterion-oriented validation procedures, and any other research procedures that allow one to predict and test something about the construct. Construct validation is especially applicable when one is dealing with difficult to measure constructs such as *ego strength, schizophrenia,* and *effective teaching.*

There are many issues underlying the application of these standard validation principles and methods to the evaluation of teaching. Some issues cut across all three approaches to validation, others are specific to one or the other validation strategy.

Common Issues

Nomothetics versus Idiographics. Nomothetics are general laws or rules that apply in a wide variety of situations. Idiographics are features of specific situations that do not generalize. In evaluating teaching, the issue of nomothetics versus idiographics reduces to a tension between the thirst for a general theory of effective teaching and the insistence that good teaching is wholly dependent on the context—which students, teachers, subjects, methods, and so on. Especially when one considers the complexity of interactions in teaching one is propelled toward the idiographic position. On the other hand, it is an axiom (and a necessity) of science that behavior is patterned and that therefore a rule can be formulated. Accordingly, one is drawn toward the nomothetic position.

A temporary solution to this issue may come from distinguishing full knowledge about teaching from adequate knowledge. Full knowledge, by definition, is situation specific. Just as the most profound knowledge about a psychotherapy patient comes from many years of daily sessions of psychoanalysis, the most complete knowledge about a teacher's teaching comes from truly extensive examination of that teacher in particular situations. Just as psychoanalysis is not necessary for all psychotherapy, however, neither is such thorough study of the teacher necessary for all evaluation. Evaluation, as psychotherapy, can proceed effectively with considerably less than total information, provided that some applicable principles can be identified and that there is room to depart from general principles when the case seems to warrant it. Thus the kinds of principles enumerated in chapters 4, 5, and 6, used in conjunction with a system of checks and balances that allows for special attention to special cases, should be adequate for virtually all evaluations of teaching.

Germane to this solution is the "cafeteria" procedure of questionnaire construction conceived, apparently independently, by Starry, Derry, and Wright (1973; see also Derry et al. 1974) at Purdue University and Flood Page (1974) in Britain. Developed first at Purdue and later at University of Illinois, University of Michigan, University of Minnesota and other institutions, this computer-based procedure effectively resolves the issue of nomothetics versus idiographics by allowing instructors to choose from a catalogue of rating items those that seem most important for their particular courses while also requiring a standard set of items to be used in all courses. To the extent that the standard items in these systems measure broadly applicable and important characteristics,[1] and to the extent that instructors can and do choose catalogue items that are truly important in their specific courses, the cafeteria procedure probably enables the most valid questionnaire-based instructional evaluations so far available.

Subjective versus Objective Approaches to Validation. The attitude of most measurement specialists for many years has been that criterion-oriented validation is the most rigorous, hence the most desirable, validation strategy. Criterion-oriented validation is indeed appealing because of its frequent use of objective tests and dispassionate statistical methods. Content validation and construct validation have been less highly regarded, content validation because of the subjectivity and possible inconsistency of expert judgment, construct validation because of its frequent abuse and subjective components. The weaknesses of content and construct validation, and the strengths of criterion-oriented validation, however, may well have been overstated. One would not want to base a theory of instruction entirely upon, say, faculty or student opinion as to what constitutes effective teaching, but a survey of world-class instructional researchers and theorists could provide exceedingly valuable information. Also, there is probably no more rigorous approach to validation than would come from the formal, empirically grounded articulation of a theory that properly applied construct validation requires. Moreover, there is a distinct possibility that the apparent objectivity of criterion-oriented validation may be misleading, for criterion-oriented validation requires numerous subjective judgments that can easily render the procedure less rigorous than either content or construct validation (for example, choice of measures, choice and application of statistics, sampling, interpretation of results; see Doyle 1977). Indeed, construct validation seems to be the method of choice for these applications not only because it subsumes both content and criterion-oriented validation, but especially because if forces researchers and teachers to think about good teaching and how best to evaluate it.

Experimental versus Correlational Validation Strategies. Experimental studies are those carried out under closely controlled conditions that involve the explicit manipulation of some critical variable. Correlational studies are typically done in the field without tight controls; they depend rather on the statistical ingenuity of the researcher to tease out relationships and causality. Experimental studies have the advantage of controlled conditions; correlational studies have the advantage of realistic conditions.

The experimental versus correlational issue in validation of evaluation is not so much the methods actually employed, because, largely as a result of Cronbach's exhortations (1957, 1975), both experimental and correlational researchers have begun to use each other's methods. The problem is more an incidental one: experimentalists read their own books and journals, and correlationalists read their own. The two literatures attack the same problems, though in different ways and often with different, albeit often complementary, emphases; yet scholars in the one camp often fail to capitalize on the work of their colleagues in the other. It is encouraging that Wittrock and Lumsdaine (1977) can suggest that the gap between the two is beginning to diminish.

Instructional Psychology versus Instructional Evaluation. A similar bifurcation exists between people who study what good teaching is and those who study how to evaluate it. Instructional psychologists, usually experimentalists, seek to identify features of the instructional setting (methods, subject matter, environment, and so on.) that bear on student learning; instructional evaluators, usually correlationists, study, for example, the reliability and validity of questionnaire and test items. Thus, both groups are interested in the same topic but each has its own way of doing things and pays unfortunately little attention to the other. There seem to be fewer signs of a merging of these two camps.

Narrow Issues

Content Validation. The key element in content validation is the choice of experts on whose judgment the estimates of item importance rest. As previously noted, a common content-validation procedure is to survey students for their judgments on the premise that they know better than anyone else how course and instructor characteristics affect them. A similar strategy is to survey faculty on the assumption that their experience in teaching qualifies them as experts. The fact that both groups tend to identify many of the same instructional characteristics as important (for instance, Hildebrand, Wilson, and Dienst 1971; Lovell and Haner 1955) provides some support for the expertise of both groups. On the other hand, this convergence can also be taken as an indication that both groups are describing a stereotype of good teaching that may have little to do with what good teaching actually entails. Although stereotypes probably have some basis in reality, to infer specific characteristics of good teachers from a stereotype is to risk misleading conclusions.

Surprisingly rare if not altogether absent in the content validation of measures of instructional effectiveness are surveys of credentialled experts: the very best instructional psychologists, rhetoricians, experts in small-group communication, and so forth; and surveys of renowned practitioners of effective teaching: the very best preachers, broadcast communicators, and trial lawyers, for example. The advantage to such surveys is not that the views of these people are any more perceptive than those of college and university faculty, but that the experts are likely to be more aware of alternatives, more conversant with the research literature, and closer to the complexities of teaching than are most faculty, and the practioners might be able to contribute fresh insights from their own successes. If nothing else, it would be worth knowing whether these two groups would have anything new to contribute.

Content validation often involves, in addition to estimates of item importance, some measure of the ability of each questionnaire item to distinguish among degrees of effective teaching, parallel to the ability of test items to differentiate degrees of learning. Test or questionnaire items that have low discriminating power are eliminated. This procedure produces an efficient questionnaire or test, that is, one with maximum discrimination and a minimum number of items. However, it also runs the risk of distracting attention from instructional characteristics that do not discriminate but that are nevertheless important. For example, if all instructors were to receive similar ratings on rapport with students, the item would probably be discarded for lack of discriminating power, but it would be incorrect to conclude that rapport has no bearing on student learning. Elimination of non-discriminating but potentially important items should be less of a problem in evaluations for promotion and salary purposes, where differentiation is the goal, than in evaluations for course improvement purposes, where it is valuable for instructors to get feedback on all characteristics that bear on student learning. Thus the situation in evaluation parallels the situation in testing, in which discriminating, norm-referenced tests are used to assign grades, and criterion-referenced mastery tests are used to assess minimum competency.

Content-validation studies occasionally culminate in a test of the selected items against student learning. Wherry (1952), for example, as already noted, selected items on the basis of expert judgment and various statistical properties: he then made up questionnaires with these items and correlated student ratings on those questionnaires with student learning gains. With the exceptions and qualifications to be described in the next section, this procedure is appropriate—but it may also be backwards. That is, it may be more efficient in the long run to base initial item selection on correlations with student learning, rather than save what many people consider the most persuasive selection criterion for last.

Criterion-Oriented Validation. Crucial to the application of criterion-oriented validation methodology is a criterion measure that is itself reliable and valid. Devising such a measure is what researchers call the criterion problem (Ghiselli 1956). In the context of instructional evaluation, there are two aspects to the criterion problem. First, the usual criterion-oriented validation study in instructional evaluation uses student achievement-test scores as the criterion. The studies seldom report the reliabilities of those tests, which is somewhat troubling; but more important, the studies rarely provide persuasive argument or documentation that the achievement test is an adequate measure of the important kinds of learning in the course, the breadth and depth of achievement that faculty seem to mean when they talk about learning as distinguished from a simple, fleeting ability to recall material. Second, an achievement test is not always an appropriate criterion for the validity of evaluations. A criterion is, by definition, an alternative measure of the same thing, as an established intelligence test might serve as a criterion for a new intelligence test, but criterion-oriented validation is frequently applied to individual evaluation items such as *clarity* and *rapport,* and student achievement is not an alternate measure of these traits. Appropriate criteria would be alternative measures of clarity and rapport, which might range from the number of ambiguous statements per unit of time to the instructor's score on a test of rapport. Once it has been determined by means of these alternative measures that the evaluation items really measure the specific characteristics they are intended to measure, then it is entirely appropriate to see if those characteristics bear on learning. The one procedure assesses the validity of the evaluation item as a measure of a particular characteristic, the other appraises the relevance of that validly measured characteristic to student learning. Both procedures are desirable, but neither one substitutes for the other. For a complementary position, see Abrami, Leventhal, and Perry (1982).

A closely related issue is the statistical model that underlies the use of achievement-test data in determining the relationship between an instructor characteristic and student learning. By far the most frequently used statistic in studies of this sort is the Pearson product-moment correlation. The Pearson correlation measures linear relationships between variables, but the assumption of linearity is not always met in these studies. The use of the Pearson correlation implies that the researcher hypothesizes, for example, that the clearer an instructor is, the more the students will learn. A competing hypothesis would have it that instructors need to be clear enough, have enough rapport with students, for learning to occur. These latter hypotheses call for threshold measures of association, not linear measures. In fact, because the application of a linear statistic to nonlinear data produces a zero correlation, the use of the Pearson correlation when a nonlinear hypothesis is tenable is not only inappropriate but also potentially misleading. Indeed, some of the lower correlations between student achievement and student ratings on particular rating items may be the result of the use of linear correlations to measure nonlinear relationships.

Another related issue is the choice of the unit of analysis. The proper model for criterion-oriented validity studies in instructional evaluation involves a multisection course in which different instructors teach similar students under similar conditions. In such a situation there are three units of analysis from which to choose. One could correlate individual ratings and test scores within the different sections, and then average those correlations across sections. This is the pooled-within-class unit of analysis, which emphasizes differences among students. A pooled-within-class analysis addresses the differential impact of instruction on students of varying backgrounds, abilities, and attitudes. In a sense it measures the potential occurrence of relationships between instructional characteristics and student learning (Doyle and Whitely 1974, Whitely and Doyle 1979). Because it emphasizes individual differences, pooled-within-class analysis may be most appropriate in instructional-improvement research.

One could also correlate mean ratings on evaluation items with mean achievement-test scores, across sections. Because computing means cancels out individual differences, this between-sections analysis minimizes student differences and describes the extent to which instructional characteristics, on the average, relate to student learning. Between-sections results portray actual relationships once the "error" of individual differences has been removed. Because it reduces individual variability, between-classes analysis may be most appropriate for research on summative judgments such as those used in personnel decisions.

Finally, one might correlate individual ratings and test scores without reference to section membership, but this total-class approach—which is probably the most common analytical model—is at best undesirable because it confounds within-class and between-class influences.

Randomization of subjects in validation studies is another problem. Most criterion-oriented validity studies in instructional evaluation involve students that have not been randomly assigned to the different section. To make these students equivalent across sections, that is, to minimize the effects of sectional differences in ability on tested learning gains, some statistical correction such as residualization is frequently employed. Leventhal (1975 and repeated personal communications) has argued that these statistical procedures are inadequate (see also Glass 1974) and that random assignment of students to sections is absolutely essential for meaningful results. Although statistical corrections are effective in principle, their application to real problems is often so complex that their effectiveness diminishes, so Leventhal is largely correct. On the other hand, the results of studies that use residualization (for instance, Doyle and Whitely 1974, Whitely and Doyle 1979, Frey 1973) seem essentially the same as those from randomized studies (Sullivan and Skanes 1974, Centra 1977), so the issue may be to some extent one of methodological aesthetics. Moreover, if one insists on randomized designs one has to forego a great deal of information about the generalizability of validity findings to various kinds of schools, diverse disciplines, different course levels, and so forth, simply because randomization is so rarely feasible. Thus there is a tension between purity and pragmatics.

One of the special complexities in residualization studies is the choice of a residualizing measure to use in adjusting initial differences in student ability. The most frequently chosen residualizing measure is the Scholastic Aptitude Test (SAT) or some similar measure of general academic aptitude. Because a residualizing test, to be effective, must be correlated with the final examination, tests such as the SAT are appropriate in courses in which what they measure is reasonably similar to (correlated with) what the final examination measures. It is not at all clear, however, that these correlations were sufficient in many of the courses in this literature to provide effective adjustment of sectional differences. Either a true pretest, parallel in content and difficulty to the final examination, or examination scores from the preceding term of a sequence course (where student motivation to do well is more likely to be similar) would be preferable.

In Leventhal's favor, too, is the fact that for effective residualization, all section differences that bear on final examination performance need to be adjusted. While the residualization studies have all tried to control for differences in student ability, they have rarely even attempted to control for differences in student motivation. One should, therefore, favor randomization studies whenever possible, but be willing to supplement their results with those of residualization studies for purposes of validity generalization.

Construct Validation. Construct validation (Cronbach and Meehl 1955) is a mightily abused concept. Rather than the rigorous articulation of interrelated hypotheses and research findings that its creators envisioned, construct validation is often an umbrella notion applied to the haphazard amassing of dubious research findings. Perhaps one reason for this state of affairs is that it is easy to advocate rigorous construct validation, but terribly difficult to apply it. In the interest of promoting the concept, the next chapter will begin developing the necessary network of testable hypotheses.

Note

1. The standard items used in the University of Minnesota version of the cafeteria procedure are "How would you rate this instructor's overall teaching ability?" and "How much have your learned as a result of this course?" See chapter 5 for explanation of why these summary items are preferable to more specific items for this purpose.

8 Toward an Overall Construct

The purpose of this chapter is to begin to spell out a network of testable hypotheses for overall teaching effectiveness. This network of hypotheses is equivalent to a rudimentary theory of effective teaching. Analogous networks—theories—could be developed for each of the specific instructor and student characteristics and each of the specific learning outcomes described in chapters 4, 5, and 6. The successive confirmation, revision, or disconfirmation of these and similar hypotheses, and the refinement of measures to which such testing would lead should result in a greater understanding of overall teaching effectiveness and a greater ability to appraise it.

It is important to emphasize that these are, for the most part, hypotheses, not confirmed research findings, and that these are only a sample of the multitude of hypotheses that could be generated.

Figure 8-1 draws together the principal evaluation focuses prescribed in chapters 4, 5, and 6. In addition, figure 8-1 indicates that attention needs to be given to teaching models, fields of study, and course format. Thus the content of figure 8-1 serves as a reminder of the factors that need to be considered in the validation of an overall teaching effectiveness construct, and the dimensional arrangement serves to emphasize the interaction of these various factors.

1. Premise. With the reservations noted in chapters 3 and 4, overall teaching effectiveness can be appraised by means of tested or rated student learning and by means of summary process ratings. The ratings may come from students, colleagues, the instructor in question, or from others. Scores from all of these overall teaching effectiveness measures should tend to converge, except under specifiable conditions.

2. Relationships among Principal Indices. The more content validity an objective-learning measure has, the more it will correlate with overall effectiveness ratings and ratings of learning. The more perceptive and forthright the raters, the more their summary process ratings will correlate with a valid objective-learning measure, provided that the raters all had sufficient opportunity to observe the instruction. The closer the relation between the instructor's and the students' judgments of which course material is impor-

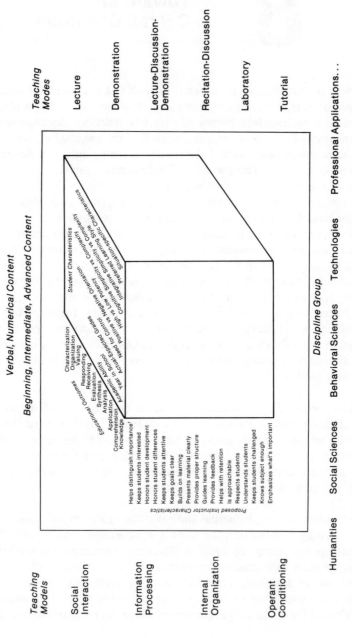

Figure 8–1. Schema for Guiding the Validation of an Overall Teaching-Effectiveness Construct

tant, the higher will be the correlation between objectively measured learning and students' summary ratings of their learning. Overall effectiveness ratings will correlate more highly with long-term retention of abstract material than with short-term recall of concrete detail. Overall effectiveness ratings from students will correlate more highly with measures of whatever learning those students consider important than with learning that they consider unimportant. The more familiar the raters are with the students in the course, the higher will be the correlation between student learning and summary ratings from those raters, provided the learning measure has good content validity and the instructor and students agree about what is important in the course.

3. Principal Indices and Rapport. Overall effectiveness scores—learning measures and summary ratings—will be higher for instructors who establish sufficient rapport with students than for those who do not. Overall effectiveness scores will be the same for instructors who establish sufficient rapport as for those who establish greater rapport, except with respect to affective outcomes. In the case of affective outcomes, effectiveness scores will be higher for those who establish greater rapport. Sufficient rapport for a given student is a function of that student's prior interpersonal experience. At a minimum, sufficient rapport means that the instructor's interpersonal behavior is not so abrasive that it distracts from learning. Instructors who demonstrate liking and respect for, and similarity to, students will receive higher rapport ratings than instructors who do not.

4. Principal Indices and Clarifying Structure. Overall effectiveness scores will be higher for instructors who provide sufficient clarifying structure than for those who do not. Effectiveness scores will be the same for those who provide sufficient clarifying structure as for those who provide greater clarification, except with certain kinds of students. Overall teaching-effectiveness scores will be lower in the case of intergratively complex and high-control students (especially when these students disagree with the instructor about course content and process) when much structure is provided than when the same amount of clarifying structure is provided for other students. Overall effectiveness scores will be higher from field-dependent students in scientific courses for whom much structure is given than from field-independent students in the same courses who are given the same amount of structure. The amount of clarifying structure sufficient for a given student is a function of that student's prior experience in the area of study and that student's stage of integrative complexity. At a minimum, clarifying structure is sufficient when the communication is intelligible and importance can be differentiated. Instructors who state intended outcomes, guide students in how best to learn the material, and point out what material is important will receive higher ratings on clarifying structure than will instructors who do not.

5. Principal Indices and Motivation. Overall teaching-effectiveness scores, whether learning measures or summary ratings, will be higher for instructors whose motivational techniques match in nature and intensity the needs of the students than for instructors who do not use motivational techniques or who use techniques that do not match the needs of the students at hand. Overall effectiveness scores will vary linearly with the amount of student-matched motivation supplied, provided that the nature of the motivational technique is not contrary to the students' needs. Motivational techniques based on testing, evaluation, and confrontation will result in higher motivational effectiveness and rapport ratings from high-potency students than from other students, but these techniques will produce lowest motivational effectiveness and rapport ratings from low-potency students. Motivational techniques based on personal relevance will produce higher motivational effectiveness and rapport ratings from negative-orientation students than from other students. Motivational techniques based on accepting students' ideas will produce higher motivational effectiveness and rapport ratings from low-potency students than from others.

6. Principal Indices and Student Ability. Overall teaching-effectiveness scores will vary less as a function of student differences in general academic ability than as a function of student differences in motivation. Overall effectiveness scores will vary more as a function of student differences in specific abilities (verbal, quantitative, perceptual, and so forth) and prior experience in the discipline than as a function of student differences in general academic ability.

7. Principal Indices and Integrative Complexity. Overall effectiveness scores will be higher from integratively simple than from integratively complex students in courses that deal in facts and principles as compared to courses that deal in higher cognitive operations. Conversely, effectiveness scores will be higher from integratively complex students in higher-operations courses. Similarly, effectiveness scores in courses that involve higher-level cognitive operations will be higher from students with more years of education.

8. Principal Indices and Control. Overall teaching-effectiveness scores will be higher from high-control students when instructors provide high clarifying structure, provided the students agree with the instructor with respect to course content and process; otherwise effectiveness scores and rapport ratings will be lower from these students than from other students.

Student need for control will moderate overall-effectiveness scores especially in courses that emphasize testing and grading, and in courses that are especially important in the academic programs of the high-control students.

9.   Compensation among Specific Characteristics. In their influences on overall effectiveness scores, exceptional skill in motivating students will compensate for deficiencies in rapport, except for low-potency students and in socially intimate courses. However, exceptional skill in motivating students will not compensate for deficiencies in clarifying structure or instructor knowledge, except in the case of students experienced in the discipline and with integratively complex and cognitively complex students; nor will exceptional instructor knowledge compensate for deficiencies in motivation, rapport, or clarifying structure.

10.   Divergence among Principal Indices. Objective learning scores will be lower than student summary-process ratings in courses that are of low-priority to those students, except in the case of generally highly motivated students and when students learned something important to them other than what was tested in the course. Student learning scores will be higher than student summary ratings when high student motivation compensates for instructional deficiencies and when motivated students consider much of the course material unimportant or contrary to their values.

11.   Relationships between Principal Indices and Specific Characteristics. Instructor characteristics, especially those relating to motivational effectiveness and providing clarifying structure, will correlate more highly with summary ratings than will student characteristics. Student motivation will correlate more highly with learning measures than will instructor characteristics or other student characteristics, except specific course-related abilities and prior revelant knowledge. Instructor characteristics that bear on motivation and clarifying structure will correlate more with learning measures than will other instructor characteristics. Student biographical variables will correlate less with summary ratings than will student ability and cognitive-style variables, and ability and cognitive-style variables will correlate less with summary ratings than will student motivational variables. Given measurement errror, relationships among principal indices of overall teaching effectiveness will account for 30–60 percent of variance. Relationships of overall measures with instructor characteristics like motivational effectiveness and providing clarifying structure, and student characteristics like motivation, will account for less variance, on the order of 10–15 percent in a multivariate analysis. Other relationships will account for still less variance.

Aside from the attention to individual differences and interactions, all of this reduces to a very straightforward conception of teaching, namely that adequate teaching requires only enough instructor knowledge, enough rapport, and enough clarifying structure to meet the minimal needs of the students at hand, while good teaching requires those same qualities plus effectiveness at motivating, stimulating, or engaging students. Complexity enters to the extent that it is necessary to determine how much knowledge, rapport, and clarifying structure is enough for particular students. It remains for further research to determine the extent to which a simple, nomothetic conception of teaching such as this one is acceptable versus the extent to which the complexity of individual differences and interactions is truly important in the practice and in the evaluation of teaching.

**Part III:
Sources**

9 Sampling

Once lists of important instructor and course characteristics and student outcomes—that is, a focus—have been arrived at, the next step in devising a procedure for evaluating teaching is to determine the acceptable and most desirable sources of information about those characteristics and outcomes.

The usual sources of information about process or outcomes in a particular course are the students, the instructor's colleagues, and the instructor himself or herself. Less usual sources of information include, among others, the subsequent employers, supervisors, and instructors of the students now in the course, former students, and specialists in instruction or instructional evaluation.

Guidance in determining which sources of information provide acceptable information and which provide the most desirable information comes from sampling theory (chapter 9), error analysis (chapter 10), traditional reliability theory (chapter 11), and generalizability theory (chapter 12).

Population and Samples

Two central concepts in sampling theory are the population and a sample. The population is the entire collection of people (or other elements) in which the researcher is ultimately interested. A sample is some subgroup of the population selected to represent that population, for reasons of convenience or economy. Any number of samples can be drawn from a population.

Precision and Bias

If a procedure applied to many samples produces essentially the same result each time, that procedure is precise. If a procedure applied to a sample produces the same result as it would if it were applied to the population, the procedure is unbiased. Thus, if one drew many samples of the student body, and if the mean student response to some evaluation question were the same each time, the data-gathering procedure would be statistically precise; and if the mean response in those samples turned out to be the same as the mean response to that item from the whole student body, the procedure would be statistically unbiased. Bias in the sampling sense should not be confused with bias in the interpersonal sense.

Precision, then, refers to fluctuation from sample to sample, and *bias* refers to how well a sample represents the population. Becasue sample-to-sample fluctuations grow smaller as the samples grow larger, precision is essentially a matter of sample size. Because random sampling virtually always results in better representation of a population than does any other kind of sampling, control of bias depends first on random sampling and second—because a random sample is truly random only if all elements respond—on response rate.

Often, the same group of people can be considered either a sample or a population. The students in a class may constitute the entire population of interest. In this case, so long as all of these students respond, there is no need to worry about precision or bias, but then one cannot generalize from these students to any others. The students in a class may also be viewed as a sample of some larger population, the whole student body, for example, or all students who have ever taken or will take this course. When the students in the course are considered a sample, both precision and bias become important.

Precision may be quantified in terms of the standard error of a statistic. If the statistic used is a mean, as is the case in many evaluation procedures, precision is quantified as the standard error of the mean: $S/\sqrt{n}$, the standard deviation divided by the square root of the sample size. The value of this quantification is that it can be used to define an interval in which the population mean is likely to fall. Because the results of many samplings from the same population will tend to form a normal distribution, approximately 68 percent of the cases will fall within one standard error of the mean, 95 percent within two standard errors, and 99 percent within three. On a typical five-point rating completed by thirty students with a mean of, say, 3.5 and a standard deviation of .8, the standard error of the mean would be $.8/\sqrt{30} = .15$. Thus the chances are 68/100 that the population mean will fall in the interval 3.5 ± .15, or 3.35–3.65; 95 percent that it will be in the interval 3.5 ± .30, or 3.20—3.80; 99 percent, 3.5 ± .45, or 3.05–3.95. In this example precision is quite good, but differences between means of less than one-half to three-quarters of a standard deviation are generally not very dependable. This illustration serves as a caution of the dangers of overinterpreting small differences on evaluations and test scores.

If the number of raters were smaller, say five, and the mean and standard deviation were still 3.5 and .8, the standard error of the mean would be $.8/\sqrt{.36}$, and the 68 percent, 95 percent, and 99 percent intervals would be 3.14–3.86, 2.78–4.22, and 2.42–4.58, respectively. This lesser precision is predictable for smaller samples and is a major problem for peer evaluations of teaching and for student evaluations in very small classes.

Sample bias is often a more difficult problem than imprecision. In the evaluation of teaching, the students in a class and the colleagues who review course materials or visit classrooms are virtually never randomly selected, so the degree to which they represent their populations, and the populations they represent, are unknown. The most one can say is that these samples generalize to populations of people "like themselves." Moreover, since the number of students that actually fill out and turn in evaluations is often smaller than the number of students in the class (response rate < 100 percent), the respondents may constitute a biased sample, even of the class. The extent of this bias cannot be determined, but it is probably greater the smaller the proportion of class members that respond and the more systematic differences there are between the class as a whole and the actual respondents (for instance, where less motivated, brighter, or more satisfied students fail to respond).

There is no rigorous procedure for determining acceptable response rate. The most one can do when faced with a significant response-rate problem is make tentative adjustments to the data, as pollsters make adjustments to their survey results. One acceptable kind of adjustment involves predicting what nonrespondents' answers would have been on the basis of answers from actual respondents who are like the nonrespondents in important known respects. For example, if the sample consists of students of various grade-point averages and years in school (both of which variables tend to show some relation to student evaluation), one can assume that the answers from higher grade-point, advanced nonrespondents would have been more like the answers from higher grade-point, advanced respondents than like those from other students in the sample. Therefore, if the proportion of higher grade-point, advanced students in the actual sample is different from the proportion in the intended sample or in the population, one can weight the results to make the sample proportions more like the population proportion. This adjustment, however, is only as valid as one's assumption that students similar in these respects will give similar evaluations.

Some adjustment is possible even if one knows nothing at all about the nonrespondents. One could, for example, construct a range of responses based on suppositions about how nonrespondents would have answered: What would the results from the total class look like if all of the nonrespondents had given the highest possible rating versus if they had given the lowest possible rating? This range would necessarily include whatever the total class results might have been, but because a range based on highest versus lowest possible ratings is often so wide as to be useless, one might prefer to set less conservative extremes, such as: What would the total class results have been if the ratio of favorable to unfavorable evaluations were, say, 10 percent more favorable among the nonrespondents than among the respondents or if the nonrespondents were, say, 20 percent more unfavorable? This procedure, too, is only as valid as its assumptions. Details on how to compute these adjustments are available in Doyle (1980) as well as in such excellent tests on sampling theory and practice as Cochran (1977), Hansen, Hurwitz, and Madow (1953), Kish (1965), and Sudman (1976).

These adjustments, however, are probably too complex for use in routine evaluations for course diagnosis and improvement, indeed for use in any but the most intricate personnel decisions.

The most important guidance that sampling theory offers to instructional evaluation is that, in sampling, both precision and bias need to be considered. Thus student evaluations from larger classes will always be more dependable—precise—than evaluations from smaller classes, and peer evaluations will always be vulnerable with respect to precision. Bias, because it is almost always indeterminate, is perhaps best dealt with by considering each set of evaluators a population in itself, refusing to generalize beyond that set, and taking pains to assure high response rates.[1] This solution makes considerable sense in the case of student evaluations and tests, because the students in the class are indeed the principal targets of the instruction; the conclusion is weaker with regard to peer evaluations, because one is usually more concerned with the judgment of the entire faculty, especially in personnel decisions, than with the judgments of a smaller number that may or may not be representative of the faculty as a whole or of any other faculty population. One could strengthen the evaluation by requiring data from more course offerings and from other sets of colleagues whenever the decisions that will be influenced by the evaluations are important enough to warrant the additional effort (for example, personnel decisions).

Note

1. However, the practice of pressing students to hand in evaluations by, for example, threatening to withhold their grades is at best imprudent, because it risks substituting interpersonal bias—negative evaluations as a result of the pressure—for statistical bias. Exhortation is generally more effective with students than conscription.

10 Error Analysis

Another way to determine which sources provide acceptable information and which provide the best is through error analysis. Error is anything that inhibits the accurate communication of an observation or judgment. Error analysis is the identification of the nature and extent of error in a communication.

Guilford's classical error analysis (1954) lists six kinds of systematic error:[1] the well-known errors of leniency, halo, and central tendency, and the less familiar logical error, proximity error, and contrast error. Leniency error is the tendency to rate too generously, especially when evaluating people with whom one is in sympathy or otherwise ego-involved. Leniency error not only results in inflated ratings, but it also reduces the ability of a rating item to differentiate among instructors, because an undue proportion of them receive the same high ratings. Halo is the tendency on the part of raters to let their evaluation of specific ratee characteristics be unduly influenced by their overall impressions of the person; the results are a blurring of distinction among characteristics and a shift in the appraisal of all characteristics in the direction of the overall impression. Central tendency is the inclination to avoid extreme judgments, to mark toward the middle of a rating scale. Central tendency reduces differentiation among instructors by placing an undue proportion in the middle range.

Among the less familiar rater errors, logical error is the propensity toward giving similar evaluations on characteristics that seem as though they should logically go together. Thus an instructor might receive unduly similar ratings on clarity and organization simply because of a subtle expectation in raters that people who are clear will also be organized. Recent studies of implicit theories of personality (for example, Hakel 1969, Schneider 1973) suggest that these anticipations may be quite elaborate, that people carry in their minds quite involved notions of how traits ought to relate to one another.

Contrast error is defined as the tendency to rate others in the opposite direction from oneself. Thus a highly organized rater might rate everyone else as less organized. A converse propensity, however, seems just as likely: some raters will describe people as unduly similar to themselves, as a very amiable rater might tend to see most people as a little more amiable than

73

they really are. Whether the error is one of contrast or similarity probably depends on the characteristic of interest and on whether the rater admires or dislikes that characteristic.

Finally, proximity error is the tendency to give more similar ratings on adjacent items on a questionnaire than on items more separated from one another. In a collection of ratings, the average rating for friendliness might be slightly more similar to the average rating for clarity when the two items are placed near each other than when they are farther apart.

Greater attention in the instructional-evaluation literature has been paid to leniency error, halo error, and logical error than to central tendency, contrast, and proximity. Leniency error in instructional evaluations, because of the lack of any objective, leniency-free criterion measure, is usually studied by comparing student, self-, and colleague ratings. Centra (1975), studying leniency error in colleague and student ratings in an institution in its first year of operation (when, presumably, an instructor's reputation would be least likely to have influenced evaluations), found colleague ratings (three colleagues each visiting the classroom twice) substantially more favorable than student ratings. On an overall instructor effectiveness item, the mean colleague rating was 4.47 on a five-point scale and the mean student rating was 3.98, a full standard deviation lower. Moreover, 94 percent of the colleague evaluations described the instructor as either good or excellent, only the remaining 6 percent as satisfactory or below. (The corresponding percentages for student evaluations were not reported.)

In another study of leniency, this one involving 343 classes in five colleges, Centra (1972) found self-ratings sometimes lower than, sometimes the same as, but usually higher than student ratings, suggesting some degree of leniency error in self-ratings (see also Doyle 1975, p. 71). He also noted different patterns of self versus student discrepancy in different curricular areas, which could mean that leniency is more likely to occur in some fields than in others. Doyle and Webber (1978a), however, found self-ratings in 146 courses in a large university generally the same as or lower than student ratings, suggesting an absence of leniency in self-ratings. Like Centra, they noted that patterns of self versus student discrepancy varied across curricula. Marsh, Overall, and Kessler (1979), studying 329 courses at the University of Southern California, found even greater similarity between self and student ratings than did Doyle and Webber. The apparent inconsistency between Centra's results and those of Doyle and Webber, and Marsh, Overall, and Kessler, may be a function of the instructors' amounts of prior exposure to student evaluations. Instructors with greater exposure may have shifted their self ratings in the direction of the student ratings. However, the data are not sufficient to confirm or disprove this hypothesis.

Doyle and Crichton (1978) studied student, colleague, and self-evaluations in an institution with a well-established evaluation program. They found less disparity between colleague and student ratings than had Centra (1975), perhaps because their instructors were better known to one another; but they found the same pattern: students tended to give the least favorable ratings, colleagues the most favorable, with self-ratings in between. Doyle and Crichton's colleague ratings tended to be more skewed toward the favorable end than either their student or self-ratings, and their student versus self-discrepancy was very close to that found in Doyle and Webber (1978a).

Sharon (1970; see also Sharon and Bartlett 1969) looked at leniency in student evaluations as influenced by the directions given to student raters and at the resistance of different rating-scale formats to leniency error. Sharon constructed a traditional numerical rating scale and a special forced-choice scale (see chapter 15), then had students rate their instructors under four different experimental conditions: (1) anonymously, with the evaluations to be used "for research purposes only"; (2) anonymously, but for use by a faculty-review committee evaluating the instructor; (3) with student identification, that is, signed by the raters; and (4) with student identification and also with the expectation that each student would later have to explain his or her ratings in a face-to-face meeting with the instructor. The numerical ratings were skewed in the favorable direction under all four conditions indicating leniency on the part of the students using the traditional scales. Moreover, the numerical ratings intended for use by the faculty-review committee and those given in anticipation of a face-to-face meeting with the instructor were significantly more favorable than those given under the other conditions. Ratings on the forced-choice scales were the same under all conditions and showed greater resistance to leniency than did any of the numerical ratings.[2]

It seems clear, then, that some degree of leniency error can be expected in most evaluations given on traditional numerical-rating scales, but that colleague ratings suffer from considerably more pronounced leniency error than do either self- or student evaluations. The degree of leniency in student evaluations does not seem to be especially great, but the degree of leniency in colleague evaluations—if Centra's (1975) results are at all typical—may be such that the usefulness of colleague evaluations is severely limited, not only because the ratings are inflated, but also because differentiation among instructors is reduced.

Determining the degree of halo error in a set of ratings is a difficult task, for it requires knowing the extent of true relationships among traits to use as a basis for assessing the extent of spurious relationships attributable to halo. It is still more difficult to compare the extent of halo error in ratings from different sources because the different ratings have different reliabilities (see chaper 10) and unreliability attenuates intercorrelations (Marsh and Hocevar, 1980).

One approach to the study of halo error in ratings has been the examination of factor structures that underlie those ratings. Factor analysis is a mathematical procedure that searches out clusters of rating items so that the items in a cluster are at once maximally correlated with one another and maximally uncorrelated with items in other clusters. Factor analysis ideally produces a set of item categories, each of which is readily interpretable and readily distinguishable from the other categories. In factor analysis of student ratings, one sometimes finds a first factor that consists of items that one would expect to appear in separate categories. Because it could be spurious intercorrelations that result in these varied items being assigned to the same factor, such factors are taken as signs of the presence of halo error (for example, in Isaacson et al. 1964). Such an interpretation is not definitive, however, because one cannot tell the extent to which the traits themselves actually were intercorrelated. Moreover, factor analysis is a subtle tool that is heavily influenced by the particular items included in the analysis, and a preponderance of high-variability items dealing with the same trait could overpower the whole set of items and result in a single mixed factor. In addition, many other influences can operate to obscure the meaning of a factor analysis (Weiss, 1970).

A more persuasive approach to the assessment of halo is found in multitrait-multimethod studies. Multitrait-multimethod research strategies attempt to appraise the reliability and validity of data by means of a detailed examination of correlational patterns involving ratings of various traits by various groups of raters (Campbell and Fiske 1959; Kavanaugh, MacKinney, and Wolins 1971). Among the many analyses under this strategy is one that looks for halo error. Doyle and Crichton (1978) found a significant amount of halo error in student and self- ratings and especially in colleague ratings (but considerably more validity than halo in each kind of ratings). Marsh, Overall, and Kessler (1979; see also Marsh and Overall, n.d.) found very similar results in their study of self- and student ratings; the evidence, however, suggested a degree of true relationship among the traits, and they concluded that some halo error exists in student ratings, little or none in self-ratings. Marsh and Hocevar (1980) applied especially sophisticated statistical techniques (LISREL modeling) to the same data and arrived at the same conclusion.

Colleague ratings, then, seem to involve the greatest halo error, and student ratings may also involve a significant amount. Self-ratings apparently suffer from little or no halo error. The degree of opportunity to observe the instructor seems to explain these results. Colleagues typically have the least opportunity to observe the instructor, students considerably more, and the instructor himself or herself the most. The more opportunity one has to observe the ratee, the more possibility there may to be make the kinds of distinctions among traits that are the converse of halo error.

One of the principal effects of halo error is that it blurs distinctions among traits. Consequently, halo error is more of a problem in evaluations for course diagnosis, where distinction among traits is important in arriving at a profile of instructional strengths and weakness, than in evaluations for promotion, tenure, and salary decisions or in evaluations for course selection and program planning, when summary evaluations are the most important. Typical colleague evaluations, perhaps because of colleagues' limited opportunity to observe the instructor, are probably of less help in course diagnosis than are either student or self evaluations.

Logical error appears in contemporary guise as implicit theories of instruction. In a study of implicit theories in student evaluations, Whitely and Doyle (1976, 1978) had some students sort rating items to produce categories of instructor characteristics and had other students rate instructors with those items. Factor analyses of the ratings and analogous latent partition analyses of the sortings produced very similar results. The fact that very similar categories emerged from ratings of actual instructors and from item sortings without reference to any particular instructor suggests that the correlation among items may arise from theories or expectations in the raters as well as from true relationships among characteristics.

However, Whitely and Doyle also pointed out that the correlational patterns in the sortings may be either legitimate or spurious, depending on their origins. Such patterns are spurious to the extent that they come from factors independent of any instructor, such as rater-response styles; they are legitimate to the extent they come from students' prior experiences with instructors, in which case the patterns can be considered acceptable anticipations of instructor behavior, and to the extent that the patterns are consistent across many instructors.

To help determine whether the patterns were spurious or legitimate, Whitely and Doyle compared the sorting categories to factors from a factor analysis of rating item means, because the means, having cancelled out individual student variability, should be better descriptors of actual instructor characteristics than were the original raw ratings. The mean-based factors were very similar to the sorting categories, suggesting that implicit theories are built on legitimate anticipations. Bejar and Doyle (1981) provide some evidence for the generalizability of these patterns across instructors.

Neither self- nor colleague ratings seem yet to have been studied for implicit theories of instruction, but because implicit theories appear to be a standard phenomenon in human perception, one can probably assume that they operate in self- and colleague evaluations as well as in student evaluations. Indeed, it may be that implicit theories, such as halo error, have more influence on perceptions the more removed the rater is from the ratee. If that should be the case, then self-ratings would be the least affected by implicit theories, colleague ratings the most.

As with halo error, the effect of implicit theories is principally on the patterns of correlations among instructor characteristics, and is therefore more likely to be a problem for diagnostic than for summative evaluations. There is no evidence, however, at this point that implicit theories, or logical error, have particularly adverse effects on evaluative ratings. In fact, Bejar and Doyle (1976) have shown that, in rating the instructor at hand, students can quite readily depart from their general expectations. The importance of implicit theories, then, may be more in the formulation of a theory of the rating process than in the interpretation of ratings data.

Similarly, the importance of contrast error, which has received virtually no attention in the instructional-evaluation literature, may be to point out the need for the study of the psychodynamics of the ratings process. It could be vitally important to the understanding and interpretation of evaluations to know whether, for example, students and colleagues do project their own deficiencies onto instructors, or if they cannot admit that instructors are imperfect. Such information could help explain generally positive or negative response styles and pave the way for understanding more about subtle instructor-student interactions. For the present, at least, it may be sufficient to assume that these propensities toward contrast or similarity error are truly idiographic and, as such, are probably distributed randomly among the raters, in which case unduly unfavorable evaluations should be cancelled out by unduly favorable ones. The danger, of course, is that a preponderance of the raters in any given group may be of similar psychological makeup, in which case, should these errors occur, they would tend all to be in the same positive or negative direction.

Central-tendency and proximity error have each received some attention in the construction of evaluation questionnaires. Central tendency is affected by the format of rating items. Because the effect of central tendency is to reduce the ability of a rating item to differentiate among instructors such that too many ratings tend toward the midpoint of the rating scale, both the number of scale points, or response alternatives, and the phrasing of those alternatives are frequently adjusted to increase differentiation. Thus rating items often have as many as six or seven (or more) scale points, and the labels attached to those points are phrased in such a way that raters will use (at one time or another) virtually the whole range of the scale. Proximity error is affected by the ordering of items on a questionnaire. Given some slight tendency for adjacent items to receive similar ratings, items measuring the same or similar characteristics will often be placed together so that, even if the distinction among aspects of the same characteristic is somewhat reduced, the distinction among different characteristics may be sharpened. Chapters 14 and 15 expand on the considerations that bear on the format of questionnaires and rating items.

Of the six kinds of error described by Guilford (1954), the ones that are most helpful in determining which sources of data provide acceptable information and which provide the best, are leniency error and halo error. The remaining errors are either mainly of theoretical interest or too slight to be really concerned about, or are quite readily controlled in the construction of questionnaires and the phrasing of items.

It is clear in the research literature that evaluations from any source, collected by means of questionnaires and rating scales, are likely to be influenced by some degree of leniency and halo error. It is equally clear that colleague evaluations are likely to contain more leniency and halo than are student evaluations, and more halo error than self-evaluations. Self-evaluations need not be influenced by leniency, but they undoubtedly sometimes are. The extent of halo error in colleague evaluations—at least in evaluations by colleagues who have had relatively little opportunity to observe the instructor—probably makes an instructor's colleagues generally the least useful source of information for the diagnosis and improvement of classroom activities. The extent of leniency error raises very serious concern about the usefulness of colleague observations of instruction for promotion, tenure, and salary decisions. The extent of leniency and halo error in typical student evaluations does not seem sufficient materially to hinder their use in either course diagnosis, student advising, or faculty-personnel decisions.

The presence of pronounced leniency and halo error in colleague evaluations does not mean that colleagues are necessarily less fair-minded or discriminating observers than students or the instructors themselves. Rather it suggests that colleagues are disadvantaged by a lack of opportunity to observe classroom instruction. Lacking this opportunity to observe, colleagues naturally give the instructor the benefit of the doubt (leniency) and find it more difficult to make distinctions among that instructor's specific characteristics (halo). On the other hand, it seems equally natural that colleagues would be more generous with one another than more distant observers might be.

The presence of leniency and halo in colleague evaluations of classroom process does not necessarily mean that leniency and halo exist in any substantial amount in colleague ratings of the scholarly foundation of the course, of course materials, or of student outcomes. Indeed, one would hypothesize that their experience in the selection and evaluation of academic materials and in the appraisal of student outcomes would make colleagues especially perceptive evaluators of these aspects of instruction, given—again—that they had had sufficient opportunity to examine them. No data exist that confirm or disconfirm this hypothesis, however.

The relative absence of leniency and halo in the student and self- ratings examined in these studies certainly does not mean that student and self-ratings are never encumbered by these errors. Sharon's (1970) study, previously examined, shows that the conditions surrounding a student evaluation can affect leniency; common sense argues that similar conditions are at least as likely to affect self-evaluations, and halo error in both student and self ratings is probably partly a function of the seriousness with which the raters approach the rating task.

Finally, there may be ways to reduce leniency and halo error in ratings, including colleague ratings. As already noted, adjustments in the phrasing and ordering of questionnaire items can reduce rater error (see Doyle, 1975, chapter 2). Sharon's study (1970) indicates that different rating-scale formats might also reduce error (for example, forced-choice scaling, see chapter 15). Work by Borman (1975, 1978, 1979) and especially Wiener (1982) generally supports this possibility. Borman (1975), however, has also pointed out that questionnaire format alone is not likely to provide maximum control over these errors and that efforts to train raters should be worthwhile. Indeed, there seems to be no reason why simply informing colleagues about the tendency toward leniency and halo error and explaining the effects of these tendencies should not significantly reduce the degree of leniency and halo in colleague evaluations. The effectiveness of training raters to reduce halo and leniency error deserves further attention.

The six systematic errors cited in Guilford (1954, chapter 11) cover most of what is usually treated as rater error in error analysis. These six kinds of error were identified by means of literature reviews, surveys of empirical-research reports. A more theoretical approach to the identification of ratings error might produce other potential errors that deserve attention. Such an approach is outlined in chapter 13.

Notes

1. Systematic error is error that is consistent in a person or a group of persons, as distinguished from random error, which is not consistent. This chapter emphasizes systematic error and chapter 11 will emphasize random error.

2. It is the patterns of ratings in studies such as Sharon's, along with the general research findings that people tend to rate other people generously (Guilford, 1954, chapter 11), that lead one to conclude that colleague and sometimes self- evaluations are unduly generous, rather than that student evaluations are unduly harsh.

11 Reliability

Traditional reliability theory is principally concerned with random error in data. Random error rises from such factors as momentary distraction, misreading of questions, carelessness, and good or bad moods on the part of individual raters as well as from poorly phrased evaluation questions and directions (see Thorndike 1967).

The notion underlying traditional reliability theory is that data are reproducible to the extent that these random errors are absent. Data may be tested for reproducibility across time, across content, and across people. Thus, ratings of the same instructor on two different occasions should be the same if the raters are not distracted, did not misread the questions, and so forth. Ratings on similar questionnaire items should be similar if random error is absent, and ratings from similar people should be similar if their evaluations are to be considered reliable. These postulates form the nucleus of a large and complex body of literature on the reliability of measurement (Nunnally 1967, Thorndike 1967, Stanley 1971).

Internal-Consistency Reliability

Internal-consistency reliability, or homogeneity, assesses the reproducibility of data by examining consistency across content: similar items or similar sets of items. Thus, to the extent that random error is absent, one should expect high correlations among ratings of, say, friendliness, rapport, and attitudes toward students, surely higher correlations among those ratings than among ratings of friendliness, organizational skill, and enthusiasm.

Student ratings of course and instructor characteristics generally show internal-consistency reliability coefficients in the .80s and even .90s, which indicates a very high degree of consistency across items (Doyle 1975, pp. 36–37). Colleague and self- ratings have been much less frequently studied than student ratings. Hildebrand, Wilson, and Dienst (1971) found homogeneity coefficients in the .60s to .80s for colleague ratings of instructor characteristics that could be evaluated without visiting classes (for example, intellectual breadth and relations with students), and Marsh and Overall (n.d.) reported internal-consistency coefficients in the .70s and .80s for faculty self-ratings. The voluminous literature on self-report personality inventories (for example, Anastasi 1976, chapter 17) suggests that self-evaluations from reasonably cooperative and insightful people are likely to result in internal-consistency coefficients of about the same magnitude as, or somewhat higher than, those reported by Hildebrand, Wilson, and Dienst (1971) for colleague evaluations.

Recent research indicates that prose (essay-type) evaluations by students are also internally consistent (Ory, Brascamp, and Pieper 1980; Brascamp, Ory, and Pieper 1981). Prose evaluations by colleagues and by instructors themselves have apparently not been studied for internal consistency.

Professionally constructed achievement tests such as the Scholastic Aptitude Test show extremely high homogeneity because these tests are explicitly built to be internally consistent. It is an open question, however, whether or not the typical classroom examination is homogeneous. Essay examinations are rarely, if ever, studied for internal consistency.

In chapter 3 a social ethic for the use of data was proposed, namely that those decisions that could potentially be the most harmful to individuals require the most rigorous data. Consequently, data intended for use in decisions about individuals (that is, promotion, tenure, and salary decisions) should probably have reliabilities in the middle .80s or above (cf. Mehrens and Lehmann 1978, p. 107); data intended for use in lesser decisions may have reliabilities as low as, say .60.[1]

Thus student evaluations and some self-evaluations seem to be adequately reliable (in the internal consistency sense of reliability) for use in all three of the major kinds of instructional decisions: course diagnosis, student advising, and faculty-personnel decisions; and colleague evaluations of nonclassroom characteristics are sometimes reliable enough for the same uses. There is apparently no evidence as yet to support or disconfirm the internal-consistency reliability of colleague evaluations of the classroom process.

Professionally constructed achievement tests are almost surely reliable enough for use in faculty-personnel decisions, but it is doubtful that the typical classroom test is reliable enough for that purpose (Mehrens and Lehmann 1977, p. 107).

To remove the doubt in specific situations, it would not be especially difficult for a statistician or psychometrician to compute the actual internal consistency of a set of colleague (or student) ratings or of an objective classroom test and thus determine whether the data are sufficiently homogeneous for their intended purpose.

Internal-consistency reliability can usually be increased quite easily in ratings and in tests. Because internal consistency is principally a function of the number of content-similar items in the questionnaire or test, with each successive item increasing the proportion of content consistency and decreasing the proportion of random error, the simple addition of more content-similar items will result in higher internal consistency. Thus a longer colleague evaluation questionnaire should help increase the reliability of colleague evaluations to an acceptable level. On the other hand, it is an empirical question how long that questionnaire would need to be and whether a questionnaire of that length would be acceptable to the raters.

Finally, it is not really essential that all tests or questionnaires be internally consistent. Higher internal consistency is important only when the instrument is composed of items that should elicit consistent responses. Most tests and questionnaires, however, are composed of such items and therefore need to meet internal-consistency standards.[2] When an instrument is not composed of items the answers to which ought to be consistent, some other estimate of reliability will be more appropriate.

Retest Reliability

The retest-reliability paradigm appraises reproducibility by studying the consistency of data over time. Evaluations have high retest reliability, or stability, to the extent that the patterns of scores from the same people remain the same on repeated testings, provided, of course, that the instructor and course have not changed in the interim. Retest-reliability studies necessarily involve an interval of time between testings; the greater the interval the more likely it is that the course or instructor will have changed and that the stability coefficient should, and will, be lower.

Because time intervals in excess of even a few days may tend to reduce stability because of changes in the course and instructor, the retest-reliability coefficient is probably a rather conservative estimate of ratings reliability. Nevertheless, stability coefficients for student ratings tend to fall in the mid-.60s to lower .80s for a variety of course and instructor characteristics, with intervals ranging from a few days to a few months (Doyle 1975, p. 39). Professionally constructed achievement tests often have stability coefficients in the .80s and above, in large part because student achievement fluctuates relatively little. No compilation of stability coefficients for classroom tests, nor any study of the stability of colleague or self evaluations, could be located.

Given the fact that stability coefficients should be regarded as rather conservative estimates of reliability, one can conclude that the reliability of student evaluations in the stability sense approximates the reliability of student evaluations in the homogeneity sense. Similarly, the stability of professionally constructed achievement tests rivals the internal consistency of those measures. No conclusions, however, can be drawn about the stability of typical classroom tests or of colleague or self- evaluations.

Unlike internal consistency, retest reliability cannot be significantly increased except by clarifying any ambiguities in item phrasing or in the instructions to raters or test-takers, because it is those deficiencies that principally interfere with stability; but stability can be more accurately appraised than in these studies. A more rigorous approach to estimating retest reliability would be to have raters repeatedly view television tapes or films of the same segment of instruction (see Borman 1978). The teaching would then be constant, and any differences in ratings would have to be attributed to the raters or to the conditions surrounding the evaluation. However, no study of this sort seems yet to have been reported in the instructional-evaluation literature.

Finally, just as not all evaluations need to be internally consistent, they do not all need to be stable. High stability is important only when the characteristic being measured is itself stable. Most course and instructor characteristics do seem to be somewhat stable, at least for short periods of time, so stability information is often useful, if not essential. When retest reliability is not an appropriate index of the absense of random error, however, then either internal consistency or interrater estimates should be employed.

Interrater Reliability

Interrater reliability addresses the question of measurement error by examining the consistency of ratings among people. Data are reliable in the interrater sense to the extent that all raters in a group give the same pattern of response.

Interrater reliability is often estimated by means of the intraclass correlation coefficient, the ratio of variability across classes to variability within classes. The notion that underlies the intraclass correlation is that there should be more similarity in a group's ratings of a single instructor than in the combined ratings of many different instructors. Doyle and Whitely (1974; see also Whitely, Doyle and Hopkinson 1973) report statistically significant intraclass correlations for virtually all instructor items in a multi-faceted student-evaluation questionnaire. Also on the basis of intraclass correlations (which are very sensitive to the number of raters, much as internal-consistency correlations are sensitive to the numbers of items),[3] Centra (1979, p. 27) predicted interrater reliabilities in the .70s for ten students, in the .80s for fifteen, and around .90 for twenty students. For similar procedures and results, see Marsh and Overall (n.d.). In a study of the comparative reliability of student and colleague ratings, Centra (1975) projected an interrater reliability of .85 for a group of fifteen students, but a reliability of only .57 for a group of fifteen colleagues.

Interrater reliability is of special interest in the grading of essay tests and the interpretation of essay evaluations, because it addresses measurement error rising from the scoring of the responses as distinguished from the responses themselves. Interrater reliabilities in the scoring of essay examinations (by about four readers) seem to cluster in the .60s and .70s, although grading by highly experienced professional graders using very structured scoring protocols may result in reliabilities well into the .90s (Coffman 1971). Ory, Brascamp, and Pieper (1980) report a mean interrater reliability of .79 for three instructional resources specialists rating students' essay evaluations, and a mean reliability of .86 for another three specialists rating students' oral evaluations of their instructor.

In the light of the reliability ethic previously described, student ratings from groups of fewer than about fifteen students are probably not reliable enough (in the interrater sense) to be used by themselves in important faculty personnel decisions. However, Gillmore, Kane, and Naccarato (1978) showed that student ratings from classes of fewer than fifteen students are likely to be reliable enough for this purpose if the ratings from at least five such classes are examined separately. (They also pointed out that if data from ten or more separate classes are examined, class size makes little difference, but that if only one or two classes are used, even large classes are not likely to provide adequate reliability for personnel decisions.) Gillmore, Kane, and Naccarato's analysis was quite complex, however, and a replication would be in order before their results should be used as more than approximate guidelines.

The most striking finding in these interrater-reliability studies is that even large groups of colleagues may not provide sufficiently reliable ratings for use in personnel decisions. If Centra's (1975) study of the reliability of colleague evaluations can be replicated, colleague evaluation of teaching, at least from an interrater consistency point of view, will have to be considered an unreliable personnel-evaluation procedure.

In the same vein, the use of essay tests and essay evaluations may be questionable in faculty personnel evaluations unless those data are scored by at least three or four judges, or possibly more. Otherwise it may be as much the proclivities of the individual raters as the content of the essays that are being communicated.

Interrater reliability is not so easily increased as internal consistency or even stability, because interrater reliability is largely a function of the number of raters that can be employed in most evaluations. Some gain in interrater reliability might be achieved by using more structured evaluation questionnaires or scoring protocols and by attempting to train raters to give more consistent evaluations. Moreover, the desirability of interrater reliability might be challenged on the grounds that highly different raters should give inconsistent ratings (see chapters 6 and 8). As matters now stand, however, the reliability of essay tests and essay evaluations remains questionable.

To the extent that all three approaches to reliability are applicable to a given set of data, the kinds of data that seem to be of acceptable reliability for use in faculty-personnel decisions are student ratings and professionally constructed objective tests, as well as objective classroom tests constructed to professional standards. There is insufficient evidence on the three kinds of reliability as applied to self-evaluations and essay examinations, although the data that do exist are encouraging. The greatest question is about the reliability of colleague evaluations, especially colleague evaluations of the classroom process, and the available data are not encouraging. These conclusions are consistent with the results of studies of halo and leniency error described in chapter 10.

From a reliability standpoint, however, colleague evaluations as well as self-evaluations, essay tests, and student essay evaluations are very probably of sufficient reliability for use in course diagnosis and improvement, but colleague evaluations in particular suffer from degrees of halo and leniency error that seriously impair their usefulness in course diagnosis.

Internal consistency, stability, and interrater reliability are the three means that traditional reliability theory provides for the estimation of measurement error. These procedures are widely used and widely respected, but none is without its critics. Chapter 12 will discuss some of the technical questions raised about traditional reliability theory and will present what some measurement specialists consider a more satisfying and comprehensive—though still imperfect—conceptualization of reliability.

Notes

1. Because reliabilities are usually based on correlations and correlations are influenced by many factors (McNemar 1969, chapter 10), these suggested levels for reliability are more on the order of guidelines than absolute requirements.

2. In questionnaires and tests that cover a wide range of topics, the requirement of internal consistency applies to each subset of items dealing with a homogeneous content. A multifaceted questionnaire or test, then, may require a number of different internal consistency coefficients rather than a single, overall coefficient.

3. Note the virtual identity between precision (chapter 10) and interrater reliability, both of which increase as sample size increases.

12 Generalizability

Cronbach et al. (1972) broadened the traditional reliability-theory concern with consistency over time, items, and people to a consideration of consistency over all conditions under which data may be collected. Cronbach and colleagues' generalizability theory thus subsumes reliability theory: if data are internally consistent, they generalize over content; if they are stable, they generalize over time; if they show high interrater reliability, they generalize over people. Generalizability theory, however, goes further: it addresses consistency over such other conditions of measurement as whether raters are anonymous or identified, whether data are collected for confidential use or for public use, whether the instructor is present or absent during the evaluation, and so forth.

Generalizability may be viewed as interchangeability. There are many different questionnaires and questionnaire items that may be used in the evaluation of teaching, many different actual and potential raters, many different times the evaluations could be collected, and many different circumstances under which the evaluation could take place. Generalizability is concerned with the extent to which different sets of these conditions result in the same information such that one set of data may be substituted for another.

Institutional policy might state, for example, that student evaluations may be collected on any of several specified ratings questionnaires, administered on any day during the last three weeks of the term except when an examination is given in the course or on the day immediately before or after a holiday, and that the evaluations be collected at either the beginning or end of a class from all students present in class at that time. Such a policy defines five categories of conditions of measurement and specifies which conditions in each category are allowable: data form (ratings, as distinguished from essay or oral evaluations), questionnaire form (the specified questionnaires and no others), medium (in person rather than by mail or telephone), time (those days and no others; at the beginning or end of the class period), and raters (students, all those present). The policy implies that variation in these allowable conditions will not affect the evaluation, that data collected under any arrangement of allowable conditions will yield the same result as data collected under any other arrangement of allowable conditions, that, in short, evaluations collected under the allowable conditions are interchangeable.

The policy, however, disregards other conditions such as who administers the questionnaires, for what stated purpose, in which of the instructor's courses, and so forth. Disregarding conditions implies that variation in the disregarded conditions will not affect the results of the evaluation.

A prerequisite to an institutional policy of this sort, then, is empirical study to determine the measurement conditions under which the evaluation results will indeed be the same and the conditions under which they will be different. Cronbach et al. describe research designs and statistical procedures to determine the consistency or interchangeability of data over measurement conditions and they offer a coefficient of generalizability analogous to a reliability coefficient to quantify generalizability.

Few formal generalizability studies of instructional evaluation have so far been reported, but many studies provide bits and pieces of relevant information.[1] This literature can be organized into studies that bear on people, those that bear on content, and those that bear on other conditions of measurement.

People

The people of interest in instructional evaluations are principally the instructor's students, the instructor's colleagues, and the instructor himself or herself. These people vary on many dimensions that might relate to the evaluations they give. As discussed in chapter 6, students differ from one another in terms of biographical variables as age, sex, and year in school; ability variables as grade-point average; and personality variables, including various academic motivations and cognitive styles. An instructor's colleagues—and instructors themselves—differ on many of those same dimensions and also in terms of academic rank, specialization within the discipline, attitude toward teaching, and so forth. In addition, student and colleague characteristics may interact with the instructor's characteristics with the result that different kinds of students and colleagues may react differently to different kinds of instructors.

Students

Chapter 6 concluded that the student characteristics most frequently related to student evaluations—that is, the charateristics over which student evaluations do not usually generalize—are year in school, academic ability, expected grade in comparison to usual grades, need for control, certain academic motivations (positive orientation toward school, negative orientation, and high versus low potency), certain cognitive styles (integrative and cognitive complexity), and perhaps a general positive versus negative outlook. When these associations do occur, however, they tend to be of only modest magnitude and therefore indicate a fair degree of generalizability across these characteristics. Thus the degree of relationship between student characteristics and student evaluations is not such that one must examine the evaluations from different types of students separately. However, these relationships do suggest that separate examinations may sometimes result in a more thorough understanding of how an instructor affects different kinds of students.

Student characteristics may also correlate with student outcomes. One would expect student abilities to correlate with either self-rated or tested student outcomes, at least those abilities that have specifically to do with the objectives of the course (for instance, quantitative but not necessarily verbal abilities in a math class). Other student characteristics may relate to outcomes and thus restrict the generalizability of outcome measures: biographical characteristics such as race or socioeconomic level may bear on students' test-taking motivation; motivational variables may override ability variables; and cognitive styles may make some kinds of test items (as well as test-item content) easier for some students, more difficult for others. In short, outcome measures may not be so generalizable as one might assume, even across nonability characteristics. The generalizability of outcome measures requires further study before conclusions may be drawn.

Colleagues

The question of generalizability is at least as pertinent to colleague evaluation as to student evaluation, because colleague perceptions are no less likely to be related to colleague characteristics and colleague and instructor interactions than student evaluations to student characteristics and student and instructor interactions. Indeed, the relatively small number of colleagues involved in most evaluations means that rater differences are likely to be more important in colleague evaluations; yet no study of the generalizability (or correlates) of colleague evaluations could be found.

For the sake of defining some potentially useful lines of research, some speculation about the generalizability of colleague evaluations over various colleague characteristics may be in order. Biographical characteristics on which colleagues may vary include age, sex, race, level of education, academic rank, field of specialization and the like, and ability characteristics including general intelligence or academic aptitude as well as more specific capacities such as verbal or quantitative facility. There seems to be no a priori reason to expect differences in evaluations according to colleague age or sex or race alone, but age, sex, and race (singly or in combination) could well be related to other colleague characteristics—for example, values—that, in turn, may relate to ratings. In an era of concern about human rights in personnel decisions (and especially in light of the doctrine of disparite impact), the interaction of rater and ratee age, sex, and race merits serious attention.

Similarly, academic rank itself may not influence evaluations, but rank may be associated with such characteristics as attitudes toward teaching, fields of study, or methods of teaching that may be associated with evaluations.

The range of colleague variability in general intelligence or academic aptitude is probably not so great that general ability is likely to relate substantially with colleague evaluations, but differences among colleagues in patterns of specific abilities (for example, verbal, quantitative) may be reflected in differences in evaluations. Highly quantitative faculty, for example, might see and value different instructor and course characteristics than do highly verbal faculty, and the evaluations they give may reflect these differences.

Field of specialization, whether considered across disciplines (for example, humanities versus natural sciences) or within a single discipline (for example, clinical versus academic nursing, experimental versus correlational psychology), seems a likely factor across which colleague evaluations may differ. Any differences in these respects may have to do with both the values and the cognitive styles that predominate in the different groups.

No less than with student evaluations, colleague evaluations may be correlated with the raters' motivational characteristics, learning preferences, and cognitive styles. Indeed, Witkin (1976) demonstrated that there are dependable differences in field dependence/independence among faculty that are associated with field of specialization and, perhaps, with values. Whether such differences would have any larger or smaller effect on colleague evaluations than their modest effects on student evaluations is an open question at this point.

Instructors Themselves

It is also of both practical and theoretical interest to know if self-evaluations of teaching vary with instructor characteristics. In the context of self-evaluations, the generalizability question is whether some instructors are more perceptive or frank than others or whether there are other instructor characteristics that need to be known before accepting a self-evaluation at face value.

The fact that some instructors rate themselves less favorably than their students rate them, while others rate themselves more favorably, and still

others rate themselves the same suggests that instructors do differ in perceptiveness, frankness, or some other salient characteristic. The salient characteristic, however, has yet to be identified with any certainty. Doyle and
Webber (1978a) tested differences in self- and student evaluations against
sixteen instructor and course characteristics and failed to find any characteristic that explained the discrepancies.[2] Centra (1975) suggests that
prior experience with student evaluations probably influences self evaluations, but that characteristic seems incidental to generalizability. Doyle
and Webber (1978b) did find that instructors with heavier teaching loads
as well as instructors who liked to teach and liked the subject matter rated
their effect on student learning more favorably than did other instructors,
but these same instructors rated their own teaching ability no more or less
favorably than other instructors rated theirs. No explicit study of instructor perceptiveness, frankness, or their correlates seems yet to have been
attempted.

Doyle and Webber (1978b) also found that instructors who said they
enjoyed teaching and liked the subject matter of the course tended to rate
themselves as more clear and stimulating, more successful in getting students interested, and more effective in helping students learn than other
instructors rated themselves, and that younger, nontenured faculty rated
themselves as more approachable; but these findings seem more germane to
construct validation than to generalizability.

Beyond the available data, one might predict that cognitive complexity
could have some bearing on self-evaluations, in that cognitively complex
instructors should tend to give ratings that vary more across traits (see
Trabin and Doyle 1981, for a parallel in student evaluations). Field-dependent instructors might tend to rate themselves more favorably on rapport
and similar items, field-independent instructors on clarity, organization,
and the like. Most instructors should rate themselves more favorably in
courses in which they are teaching students they like and who like them and
with whom they feel well matched (see Uranowitz and Doyle 1978). The
generalizability of self evaluation, however, like the generalizability of colleague evaluations, is for the most part uncharted territory.

Across Sources

If evaluations are similar enough across students, colleagues, and the
instructors themselves, the data from one source may be substituted for the
data from another (for example, colleague evaluations for student evaluations).

Numerous studies have compared student evaluations to colleague or
self evaluations, and an occasional study has examined all three simultaneously. There appears to be some convergence of data from the three

sources, especially student and self- evaluations, and especially with respect to the pattern of the instructor's strengths and weaknesses (strongest point, next strongest, and so forth).[3] However the data clearly indicate that colleague and student evaluations cannot substitute for one another, nor can colleague and self- evaluations (see Doyle 1975, pp. 71–72). Self- and student evaluations tend to be more similar, but the extent of the similarity is not always such that these sources should really be considered interchangeable (for example, Doyle and Webber 1978a, and Marsh, Overall and Kessler 1979). Indeed, some of the similarity may be due to the instructor's prior experience with student evaluations (Centra 1973).

Evaluations from current students have occasionally been compared to evaluations from former students, or alumni. Evaluation from these groups tend to be quite similar (Drucker and Remmers 1951, Centra 1974) but the studies are inconclusive because there is no way of knowing the extent of any change in the instructor since the former students had last had the opportunity to observe him. In any event, the logistics of collecting alumni evaluations makes it unlikely that those data will be used much in the routine evaluation of teaching. Perhaps the most noteworthy point about these alumni studies is that they are not consistent with the hypothesis that alumni, owing to their greater maturity and broader perspective, will give more favorable evaluations (Doyle 1975, pp. 72–73).

Content

Generalizability of content has to do with the internal consistency or equivalence of questionnaires and questionnaire items.

The many factor-analytic studies of student rating questionnaires (summarized in Doyle 1972, chapter 2) show high internal consistency for items within factors or content categories as expositional clarity and rapport, less, but still considerable, internal consistency across categories. Thus from a psychometric point of view, rating items within content categories can often be substituted for one another (*clarity* for *organization,* for example), and one could make an argument that quite a few items are interchangeable across categories. However, some of this internal consistency is almost certainly due to halo error, which inflates item intercorrelations (see chapter 13) and may blur distinctions among instructor characteristics, so it would be poor practice to attempt to interchange items within factors without regard to their semantic content—*clarity* is not semantically the same as *organization*—and poorer practice still to exchange items across categories. Slight differences in the phrasing of items probably have little or no influence on the results of the evaluation, however.

Also from a purely psychometric point of view, the means of ratings across many specific items might often be substituted for a general item such as overall teaching ability. The risks in this practice, however, are that computing the mean treats all items as equally important (unit weighting) and that across different questionnaires a given subset of items might generally elicit more or less favorable ratings and therefore bias that mean in comparison to the means computed on other sets of items. It is simpler and less risky to use the single summary item.

Just as two or more forms of an achievement test can be made psychometrically equivalent (see Nunnally 1967, pp. 181-186), so too—in theory at least—can different forms of an evaluation questionnaire. One would continue revising the questionnaire items until, when the same raters rate the same instructors with the different questionnaires, the means, standard deviations, and item intercorrelations are identical. There seems to be little practical reason for such an exercise, however, and considerable risk of measurement error. Moreover, this procedure would again disregard the semantic content of the items on the different forms.

Other Conditions of Measurement

Of the multitude of other conditions that may have a bearing on instructional evaluations, those that have been studied thus far include whether the raters are anonymous or identified, what the stated purpose of the evaluation is, when the evaluations are collected, and what the social climate of the classroom was at the time of the evaluation.

The literature does not support the common assumption that identified students will give more favorable evaluations than anonymous students (Sharon 1970, Stone, Spool, and Rabinowitz 1977). One could argue either, then, that student evaluations ought to be identified, out of respect for the common-law tradition that witnesses be known, or that they ought to be anonymous, to reduce the likelihood of *quid pro quo.* The latter seems the wiser choice, especially with regard to vulnerable graduate and professional-school students, if for no reason other than to protect them against retaliation by the occasional ineffectual and unscrupulous instructor. There seems to be no literature on the anonymity of colleagues evaluating course materials, and anonymity would be difficult to maintain for colleagues visiting classrooms, for students taking final examinations, and for instructors doing self-evaluations.

The literature is not consistent about the effects that different purposes of evaluation may have on student evaluations. Sharon (1970) found clearcut differences between evaluations collected for research purposes only and those that were to be used in personnel decisions, but Centra (1976) found very little difference between student ratings gathered for feedback purposes and those for use in promotion and tenure decisions. Sharon's more pronounced differences may have been the result of his more dramatic experimental manipulation, but Centra's differences might have been greater had the instructors about whom the personnel decisions were to have been made attempted to play on the sympathies of students. It is also possible that the quality of teaching mediates these effects: raters are probably more tempted to be lenient when they are giving unfavorable ratings, otherwise there is no need for leniency.

There is no explicit literature on this topic for colleague evaluations, but Centra's (1974, 1975) finding of marked leniency error in colleague evaluations suggests that different purposes of evaluation are at least as likely to influence colleague evaluations as student evaluations. One would expect, although there are probably exceptions, that self-ratings would tend to be more favorable the more important the decision. Objective-learning measures, of course, are unlikely to be affected by this phenomenon, except insofar as students might be persuaded to try harder if their performance were to have a bearing on a favored instructor's career development.

It is possible to collect evaluative data any time during a course. Bejar and Doyle (1976a) found statistically significant similarities between student evaluations collected at the end of the first class period and those collected six weeks later, but surely not enough similarity to warrant substituting one set of data for the other. Frey (1976) mailed evaluation questionnaires to students so that half the class received them at the beginning of the last week of the term, the others during the first week of the following term. There were no differences in the two sets of evaluations. (Frey's results indicate not only that student evaluations are stable but also that the final examination, which took place in the interim, did not affect the data.) The stability coefficients discussed in chapter 11 also indicate that student evaluations are very consistent over time. From a measurement point of view, then, it does not seem to matter much when student evaluations are collected, as long as the students have had enough exposure to a representative sampling of the course. What is lacking, however, is specific information on how much exposure is enough and how variable teaching is from class session to class session. Common sense suggests that summative evaluation takes place toward the end of the course, formative evaluation at any time, preferably quite early; common sense and reliability coefficients indicate that students typically do have enough exposure to give reliable ratings. As usual, there are no empirical data available to guide the timing of colleague or self-evaluations.

One could hypothesize that certain events outside the classroom could have a bearing on student, colleague, or self- evaluations. Thus the day before or after a major event—on some campuses a football game, on most, holidays—might not be a good time to collect student evaluations. Similarily, the busy weeks at the end and at the beginning of the term are probably not a good time for any formal evaluations. Common sense will again have to govern.

A final set of conditions are those that define the social context of the evaluation. The social-psychology literature supplies abundant evidence that perceptions—and therefore ratings—can be influenced by the social milieu (for example, Schachter 1967, Abrami, Leventhal, and Perry 1982). Thus an instructor's demeanor before or during a student or colleague evaluation may unduly influence ratings, so evaluations collected by the instructor may not always be interchangeable with those collected by a proctor. In a similar vein, Ward, Clark, and Von Harrison (1981) demonstrated that student evaluations are more favorable when an instructor's colleagues are visiting the classroom than when only the instructor and students are present, perhaps because the mere presence of the colleagues energized the students, more probably because the presence of the colleagues energized the instructor. Just as individual intelligence and personality tests can be affected by the examiner's rapport with the examinee (Anastasi 1976, p. 34–37), rapport between proctor and students, or among students, or among colleagues may influence the results of an evaluation.

Of the conditions of measurement so far studied, those that seem most likely to influence ratings, and hence to limit generalizability, are those that bear on the social context of the evaluation. Social influences seem likely to affect evaluations from all three principal sources—students, colleagues, and the instructors themselves. Some serious attention to the standardization of the conditions surrounding an evaluation is therefore warranted. Chapter 17 will address this issue in more detail.

Notes

1. Exceptions include Gilmore, Kane, and Naccarato (1978).

2. Age, sex, whether tenured or not; years of teaching experience, teaching load; enjoyment of teaching, liking for the subject; class size; and eight others of these sorts.

3. Convergence of evaluations from different sources is often taken as evidence of validity. It can also be taken as evidence for interrater reliability. Thus generalizability theory subsumes not only traditional reliability theory but part of validity theory as well. Note the potential for blending generalizability theory and construct validation to provide a well articulated, testable theory of data.

13 Toward a Process Conception of Reliability

Neither reliability theory nor generalizability theory makes much explicit reference to the process of evaluating, to the mental steps through which a rater proceeds in determining and communicating an evaluation. Error analysis pays somewhat more attention to process phenomena in its consideration, for example, of the origins of halo and logical error, but it still focuses principally on the result of the process. In general, with the exception of Wherry's (1952) theory of rating and Saal, Downey, and Lahey's more recent work (1980), researchers have paid little attention to the process of evaluating.

The advantage to an examination of the evaluation process is that such an examination may generate hypotheses likely to be overlooked by traditional reliability and generalizability theories, and by error analysis, especially hypotheses that bear on the relative strengths and weaknesses of evaluations from the different sources of information. In addition, it is possible that a consideration of the process may force some reassessment of traditional theories of measurement. As in chapter 8, the ideas expressed here are for the most part hypotheses, not facts.

One can begin an analysis of the rating process by examining the four elements of any evaluation: the ratee, the rater, the evaluation item, and the context in which the evaluation is performed (Crichton and Doyle 1976a, 1976b). The ratee is the stimulus. He behaves or is, and his behaviors and characteristics are to some degree observable by the rater. The rater is the most active element. He experiences the ratee, formulates judgments or observations, and communicates them. The evaluation item focuses the rater's attention and elicits a particular observation or judgment, and throughout the process, the context impinges on both ratee and rater.

The rater's functions in the evaluation process include sensing, perceiving, reinterpreting, evaluating, and communicating. He senses the stimulus—the instructor—viewing and listening to the ratee's observable behaviors and characteristics. Because of the operation of the selective-attention mechanism (James 1890), the rater attends to only a small portion of the information he encounters. This mechanism could possibly account for some differences among student, colleague, and self evaluations. For example, the personal histories of the individual raters (of whatever group) may sensitize some raters to some instructor behaviors or characteristics, other raters to others. Moreover, the teaching experience of faculty may help them attend more than students do to instructor behaviors and characteristics that are usually considered important. Similarly, the personal awareness and prior evaluation experience of the instructor may direct the rater-instructor's attention to aspects of his own teaching to which he is especially sensitive, and each individual student or type of student may have a history that affects the attention he or she gives to particular instructor and course characteristics and behaviors.

The less experience a rater has with evaluation, the greater effect selective attention seems likely to have: for better or worse, repeated encounters with evaluation questionnaires should gradually lead the rater to attend more to the characteristics tapped by those questionnaires than to other course and instructor characteristics. Raters' expectations, stereotypes, or metatypes (Bejar and Doyle 1976b, 1976c; Whitely and Doyle 1976) are likely to have a similar effect. Raters' tendencies to remember more clearly those things they encounter first or most recently (the so-called primacy and recency effects; cf. Horton and Turnage 1976, chapter 4) or to remember good experiences versus bad experiences (cf. Freud 1914, p. 45) may further delimit what the raters attend to. Halo and logical error, which perhaps interact with field dependence and cognitive and integrative simplicity, may also influence the rater's function at this stage of the evaluation process.

At the next stage in the process, the rater combines his past and present information about the ratee with information about himself and his physical, social, and psychological environments. That is, he transforms what he has sensed into a perception. Among the important processes at this stage is the development of historical composites and internal norms. These composites are the rater's recollection of his past and present observations and judgments of the instructor at hand. The norms are experience- or theory-based conceptions of what good teaching is or should be, to which the rater compares his recollection of the instructor.

Characteristics of the rater and the rating situation should influence both the composites and the norms. In the formulation of a composite the rater searches his memory for representative—or perhaps nonrepresentative but especially significant—experiences and then blends these experiences into a single conception of the instructor. The more experience the rater has with the instructor, the more dependable those conceptions are likely to be. Hence students probably have the advantage over colleagues in the evaluation of their own instructor, though colleagues may have the advantage in the determination of what constitutes good teaching in general.

In the development of internal norms, the greater experience that advanced students have with college teaching should make their norms more dependable than those of less experienced students. Less experienced students should incline more toward idealistic norms, more experienced students toward realistic ones. Student ability, need for control, motivations, and cognitive styles should also influence these conceptions of good teaching, in that students are likely to define good teaching in terms of the characteristics and behaviors of teachers who most closely meet their own particular needs. Finally, halo and contrast errors should exert their influences at this stage too, as should any special pleasantness or unpleasantness surrounding the evaluation situation.

In the case of colleague ratings, greater amounts of teaching experience, especially experience in teaching courses and students like those of the instructor at hand, might have either of two effects. Greater experience might lead a colleague to recognize multiple norms, various equally desirable ways of teaching; or it might lead him to develop a clear vision of the "one right way" to teach this course. The colleague's own personality (for instance, integrative complexity, need for control) probably determines which of those effects will occur.

Colleagues' personal characteristics probably also influence their conception of what good teaching can or should be, but the case with colleagues is different from the case with students. In the case of students, the extent to which the instruction is tailored to the students' characteristics may define good teaching, so relationships of evaluations with student characteristics may be legitimate. However, because colleagues are not the targets of instruction, relationships between their conceptions and evaluations of teaching and their personal characteristics are legitimate only in the rather unlikely case that the colleague is personally very similar to or exceedingly empathic with the typical student. An inherent difficulty with colleague ratings of classroom presentation is that colleagues must always infer how an instructor's teaching will affect students.

The social circumstances surrounding the evaluation are just as likely to affect colleague evaluations as student evaluations. In colleague evaluations, however, the social circumstances are less likely to be those of the classroom, more likely those of the department itself. Just as the politics of grading may sometimes influence student evaluations, the politics of day-to-day academic life may influence colleague evaluations. Which influence is the greater would be specific to the situation and could be very difficult to determine.

In the evaluation process thus far, the rater—whether student or colleague—has developed his own conception of what good teaching is or should be and has formulated his summary vision of the instructor at hand. This formulation may be latent, however, needing some explicit question to elicit it.

At the next step, then, the rater is presented with an evaluation question. He reads (senses) that question and interprets (perceives) it. This reading and interpretation is first affected by any ambiguity in the question, by any momentary distraction, and possibly by any selective perception or unconscious but meaningful misperception on the part of the rater. In addition, the more subjective or inferential is the instructor characteristic described in the question, the more likely it is that the rater's personal characteristics and history will influence his or her interpretation of the evaluation question.

Finally, the rater must hold on to his interpretation of the evaluation item, bring forth his composite perception of the instructor, and reinterpret that perception to conform to the requirements of the question. He must select from his composite perception only those elements that bear on the aspects of instruction he understands are relevant to the question, organize them with respect to the dimensions of his theory of teaching, and compare them to his internal norms. In addition, he must determine the strength of any reservation he may have (probably on the basis of recent social experience) about the ratee, the item, or his tentative evaluation, and decide how, if at all, that reservation should affect his ultimate evaluation. Last, he must communicate the evaluation either orally or in prose or by means of some quantitative assignment of the ratee to an item category or to a position on a scale.

During this final stage of the rating process, the evaluation may be influenced by the rater's memory of instructor and course behaviors and characteristics, by the rater's thoughtfulness, by his wisdom in determining which particular traits or behaviors merit special weight, by any intentional leniency or harshness, and by any carelessness or inattentiveness in marking the rating on the answer sheet. With respect to some of these qualities, student raters probably have the advantage, with regard to others, colleagues. Students, for example, by reason of the sheer number of questionnaires they complete and perhaps from a relative lack of appreciation for the seriousness of the rating task, may be more likely than an instructor's colleagues to be inattentive, cursory, and careless. Colleagues, on the other hand, seem more likely than students to be lenient, but they may also, by virtue of their greater experience with teaching, be more likely to have developed an alertness and memory for the salient aspects of teaching.

Even this rudimentary outline of the rating process seems heuristic in that it has led to some hypotheses that have apparently been overlooked within more traditional frameworks, such as the potential influence on evaluations that might rise from individual differences in selective attention and in the formation of raters' composite perceptions of the ratee. A more detailed outline may produce additional testable hypotheses.

This process concept has also touched on two phenomena that are not usually addressed in reliability theory or in error analysis: the likelihood of legitimate differences among raters in the evaluations they give to the same instructor, and the extent to which an evaluation is a function of both the rater and the ratee.

In traditional reliability theory, any departure from the group mean (as the best estimation of the "true" amount of the characteristic in question) is considered error. The process conception, however, underscores the likelihood that the different personal histories of raters will lead to different experiences with the same instructor and hence to legitimately different evaluations. On the other hand, the process conception also makes clear that many points at which error may influence evaluations. The researcher's task, then, is to distinguish (and quantify) legitimate, even desirable, variation from variation due to error.

One route to this end becomes apparent when the ratings of a class of students or a team of colleagues are pooled to form a composite. If the composite evaluation is left undifferentiated, any variation around the group mean will generally be considered error. If, however, one finds that within the overall group there are various identifiable subgroups, that is, smaller sets of raters that are similar to one another in characteristics that relate to their ratings and at the same time different in those same respects from the members of all other subgroups, then it becomes possible to examine the evaluations from the different subgroups separately (chapter 6) and to consider as error only those presumably more limited departures from the subgroup mean. Direct support for this line of thinking can be found in Overall's (1965) and LaForge's (1965) factor-analytic studies of ratings, in Tucker and Messick's (1963) work on points-of-view analysis, and in Carroll and Chang's (1970) research on individual differences and multidimensional scaling. More general support comes from the notion of aptitude-by-treatment interactions (Cronbach and Snow 1977). Indeed, of the approaches to reliability discussed in these chapters, only generalizability theory, a logical extension of trait/treatment interaction thinking, seems readily able to deal with legitimate differences among raters.

In traditional reliability theory, there is also the presumption that the trait at hand resides exclusively in the ratee. Reliability theory's principal focus is the fidelity with which this ratee characteristic is measured. In the process conception, however, it becomes evident that raters' different backgrounds and needs may be so intimately associated with some of their experiences with and evaluations of the instructor that one can argue that the characteristic resides in both the ratee and the rater. In this respect, Ghiselli and Ghiselli (1972) point out that some characteristics are more inferential, more subjective, than others and that the more inference there is required of the rater, the more the rating can be considered a joint function of the two.

Traditional reliability theory works quite well for low-inference qualities such as height and weight, but it breaks down with progressively more subjective qualities as clarity of exposition, rapport, and overall teaching ability. Generalizability theory may be able to deal with this phenomenon, but does not especially help one recognize it.

In a practical sense, there may be nothing necessary except to adjust one's interpretation of evaluations to account for this dual residence of most instructor and course characteristics. In fact, because a goal of teaching is to reach the students in one's particular course, it is probably more desirable to conceive of instructional qualities as partly the instructor and partly the student rather than solely as qualities of the instructor. Thus clarity alone is less important than clarity with these particular students.

This process concept also seems to differ from both reliability theory and generalizability theory in terms of the quantification of research results. Both reliability theory and generalizability theory attempt to summarize their estimations of the fidelity of measurement by means of a single coefficient. The reliability coefficient is the ratio of true (or systematic) variance to total variance, and the analogous generalizability coefficient is the ratio of universe-score variance to expected variance. The quantity and variety of possible sources of error identified by the process approach suggest, instead, a planned series of studies of the fidelity of ratings, different studies for the various principal opportunities for error. The results of these studies would not be reported as a single coefficient, but rather as a set of research results to be interpreted the same way one interprets a set of validity results. Indeed such a planned series of studies may be to reliability what Cronbach and Meehl's (1955) network of testable hypotheses is to validity.

Finally, a process model of evaluation might lead eventually to a more rigorous and realistic, though perhaps less aesthetically appealing, framework for assessing the quality of data. The payment exacted for the mathematical elegance of reliability and generalizability theories as applied to ratings, or for that matter of any theory of ratings data built entirely on consistency, is the awkwardness of dealing with some kinds of consistency and the isolation of working in an essentially solipsistic system. Traditional reliability theory proposes that all nonsystematic variation is error and that all variability that is not error is true or good. Similarly, generalizability theory implies that increased consistency results in increased dependability. The problem in applying these consistency models to ratings data is that ratings are vulnerable to some kinds of undesirable consistency. Halo effect, for example, adds to the consistency of ratings across traits, but diminishes the real discreteness of those traits. Similarly, leniency error increases the consistency of ratings across instructors by reducing real differences among them. When the fidelity of ratings is assessed by either internal consistency or stability procedures, and when generalizability is described by procedures that measure variation along item and instructor facets, the resulting coefficients are inflated by these kinds of undesirable consistency.[1] The planned series of studies that should grow out of a process view of ratings could deal with this problem by designing research that addresses both desirable and undesirable variation in the same body of data. It may also be possible to devise reliability and generalizability coefficients that correct for undesirable variation, perhaps through analysis of variance techniques applied to multitrait-multimethod data.

Reliability theory especially can be considered solipsistic in that it deals only with patterns of variability in a body of data without any explicit effort to relate that consistency to a reality outside the body of data. While this may be simply the result of an artificial but enduring distinction between reliability and validity, it nevertheless leads to a rather ethereal and unsatisfying assessment of ratings data. Just as Cronbach and Meehl's (1955) construct validation requires some explicit connection with empirical reality, the appraisal of fidelity at each step of the rating process should lead to an assessment of data quality that is less a system unto itself.

Note

1. Brown's distinction (1976, p. 63) between valid and invalid systematic variation is a rare theoretical recognition of this problem.

Part IV:
Instrumentation

14 Fluid Instruments

The instruments of instructional evaluation are the devices through which questions are asked and answers given. These instruments can be arranged on a continuum from subjective to objective, fluid to fixed: conversations, letters, essay questionnaires, rating scales, and tests. With the former, respondents use their own words to communicate their observations and evaluations; with the latter, they use somebody else's words and communicate by checking boxes or circling numbers. Each of these different forms of communication has its own advantages and disadvantages.

Conversations

Conversation may be the most potent—and least used—method of evaluation for course diagnosis and improvement. It is perhaps the most potent because it is only through conversation, dialogue, and discussion that issues can be formulated in a common language; that an unlimited survey of the strengths and weaknesses of a course can be made; that diverse points of view can be raised and promptly clarified, challenged, and revised; and that promising steps toward improvement can be formulated, agreed on, and initiated by all parties simultaneously. Conversation is the method of evaluation that seems most likely to promote understanding.

The free form and intimacy of conversation, however, may be the very qualities that make it so little used: an open discussion of an instructor's strengths and weaknesses is threatening to all participants. Experience with evaluative conversation coupled with sensitivity and worldwise discretion should help to reduce this anxiety.

Maier (1952, cited in McKeachie 1978, chapter 5) describes a structured discussion technique that seems especially promising for use in course diagnosis and improvement. The essence of Maier's developmental-discussion strategy is that a problem is presented in such a fashion that all discussants address the same aspect of the problem at the same time. In an evaluation context the problem might be, How can students become more engaged in this course? The outline of the discussion resembles any diagnostic or problem-solving procedure:

1. Formulate the problem
2. Suggest hypotheses
3. Procure relevant data
4. Evaluate alternative solutions.

The discussion leader might approach the first step by suggesting separate examination of the instructor's role, the students' role, the role of the textbook and other course materials, and so forth. For each of these components separately, the leader would guide the discussants through Maier's four-stage procedure.

Borman and Borman (1972), and Borman et al. (1982) provide a complementary analysis and suggest techniques and exercises for facilitating interpersonal communication.

Parent, Vaughn, and Wharton (1971) also propose an approach to instructional evaluation that centers on group discussion. To elaborate somewhat on their proposal, all of the students in a small class, or a committee of students from a larger one, might meet regularly with the instructor to discuss the teaching in the course. The students might be volunteers, or they could be drafted; they might be the same students each time, or the committee could have a revolving membership. The conversation could be free form, or it could proceed along the lines of Maier's method. The important thing is that the instructor and the students have the opportunity to discuss the course freely and constructively. In addition, the students who comprise this committee could also act as liaisons between the rest of the class and the instructor, bringing to the discussion any suggestions, compliments, and complaints communicated to them by the other members of the class. This liaison function could help to reduce some of the anxiety that might be associated with meetings of this sort in that a student could easily present his or her own complaint as that of someone else.

The principal disadvantage of conversational evaluations is that they cannot be readily tabulated, normed, or even recorded for later use. In addition, group dynamics might sometimes bias the direction and flavor of the discussion (see, for example, Asch 1956). Hence conversational evaluation is probably not appropriate in evaluation for faculty-personnel decisions or for course selection.

One final advantage to conversational methods of evaluation is that they might help solve one of the enduring problems in student evaluation of teaching—keeping students interested in the evaluation—by actually engaging them in the process and by demonstrating that their observations are indeed receiving attention.

Letters

Letters of compliment or complaint from a student or a colleague to the instructor or an administrator were once a principal evaluation form. Like any anecdotal report, such letters were (and probably still are) very powerful determinants of an instructor's reputation in the eyes of administrators.

Evaluative letters should be considered at best supplementary to more systematically collected data because these letters too easily give undue weight to isolated cases. The views of one or two especially satisfied or dissatisfied (and assertive) students or colleagues should not be permitted to outweigh more representative evaluations, and occasional letters should certainly not be substituted for more systematic evaluation.

On the other hand, thoughtful letters do provide some information, and very thoughtful letters can provide a great deal. An experienced teacher described a situation in which a single letter had a strong positive influence on his teaching (Clyde Parker, personal communication). In this instance, a colleague asked if he might sit in on the instructor's class to update himself about the course material. The instructor seized this opportunity to ask for an evaluation from the colleague. The colleague agreed, provided that he could study all of the course materials, examine student evaluations of the course, and even interview the students. This process resulted in a lengthy letter from the colleague to the instructor, analyzing the course, stating hypotheses, marshalling evidence, and proposing steps that could improve the course—in short, a letter framed along the lines Maier recommended for developmental discussion. Although this evaluation may have been unusual for its thoroughness, it is not beyond reason to expect that similar opportunities might arise from time to time.

Questionnnaires

Questionnaires—structured inventories of observation and opinion answered in the respondents' own words—exist on a middle ground between open-ended conversations and letters on the one side, and fixed-response rating scales and tests on the other. Questionnaires often allow respondents to address issues that might not be tapped by closed-ended instruments. Their structured quality allows the person who prepares the questionnaire to ask what he or she considers important, but the open-ended form allows respondents to direct their comments where they choose. Questionnaire responses can be shown to other people and filed for later use, but they are difficult to tabulate, cannot be normed, and are vulnerable to irrelevancy and ambiguity of response. Eliciting detailed responses can be difficult, and penmanship can be a problem.

The phrasing of items is at least as important in evaluation by questionnaire as the structuring of discussion is in conversational evaluation. Some guidance in question-phrasing can be found in the survey-research literature (for example, Moser and Kalton 1972, chapter 13; Oppenheim 1966, chapter 3; Berdie and Anderson 1974). Additional help is available in books and articles on classroom testing, especially essay testing (for instance, Gronlund 1981, chapter 9; Mehrens and Lehmann 1978, chapter 8; Coffman 1971).

Prescriptions derived from both these literatures include:

1. Write focused questions rather than broad, inclusive ones.
2. Ask respondents to write about only what they know about and are willing to discuss.
3. Use vocabulary and writing style appropriate for the respondents.
4. Have someone else review the questions before you use them, preferably a number of people from the population you are surveying.
5. Revise the questions on the basis of experience.
6. Use as few questions as will do the job.

Careful scoring of questionnaire data is essential to an accurate interpretation. Procedures recommended for scoring essay examinations are just as applicable to questionnaires:

1. Read all respondents' answers to one question before going on to the next question.
2. If desired for a record or for greater precision, especially in personnel decisions, quantify each question by translating the response into a rating (for example, five points: poor, fair, good, very good, excellent.
3. If the data are to be used in important decisions, have the answers read and tabulated by *at least* two competent readers in addition to the instructor.

Data from conversations, letters, and questionnaires are no more or less valid than the topics they address, and no more or less dependable than their sources. Accordingly, greatest attention in the interpretation of these data needs to be given to narratives about the kinds of course and instructor characteristics described in chapter 5 and to evaluations by competent and forthright people who have had at least sufficient opportunity to observe what they are describing (chapter 11). Conversations and letters, because they involve so few respondents, are especially likely to be encumbered by respondent differences and situational influences (chapters 6 and 12). Fluid evaluation instruments by their very nature are difficult to employ in faculty-personnel decisions, but they may be the instruments of choice in course diagnosis and improvement.

15 Ratings

Rating scales are probably the most widely used instruments for collecting observations and opinions. In the evaluation of teaching, the advantages of ratings are (1) they can be easily tabulated, statistically analyzed, normed, and stored; (2) they are efficient in that large amounts of information can be collected quickly and inexpensively; (3) they are highly structured, so one can ask for precisely the information one wants and elicit the same information from every respondent; and (4) there is a large body of technical literature to guide their construction and use.

Ratings have important disadvantages too. Because they are so highly structured, they do not necessarily allow respondents to convey the subtlety or entirety of their thoughts; because they are so easy to answer, they may not encourage reflection and thoughtful responding; and because they are so widespread, they may be seen as tedious, repetitive, and marginally relevant to the course at hand. Moreover, they do not always facilitate dialogue, indeed may become a substitute for dialogue. Nevertheless, either by themselves or in conjunction with some other information-gathering device (for instance, questionnaires, conversations), rating scales will and should continue to play a major role in the evaluation of teaching. For this reason, an extended discussion of the principal types of rating scales is warranted here.

Graphic, Adjectival, and Numerical Scales

These are the most frequently encountered scales. Graphic scales consist of a labeled line on which the respondent puts a mark at any point to communicate a rating:

				x
Poor	Fair	Good	Very Good	Excellent

Although graphic scales permit very fine gradation of traits (since the rater's mark may be put at any point on the continuum), they are rarely used in large-scale or routine evelation programs because they are more difficult to tabulate than adjectival or numerical scales.

Adjectival scales consist of an ordering of adjectives or adjectival phrases, one of which the respondent circles:

Poor   Fair   Good   Very Good   Excellent

These scales permit distinctions as fine as the adjectives themselves, gross distinctions such as *good* versus *bad* or fine distinctions such as *fairly good* versus *good*. It is important that the adjectives form an unequivocal scale, that is, a clear ordering from good to bad (or the reverse), much to little, infrequent to frequent, and so forth, and that the semantic differences between pairs of adjacent adjectives be approximately equal (*poor/fair/good* versus *poor/fair/superb;* Guilford 1954, chapter 11). In the absence of a clear ordering, the results will be misleading; in the absence of equal intervals, analysis is limited to lower-order, nonparametric statistics (Siegel 1956).

Numerical scales simply add numbers to adjectival scales:

Poor   Fair   Good   Very Good   Excellent
 1   2   3   4   5

Sometimes just the numbers are presented, with a separate key for definition. In either case, the presence of numbers makes keyboard-based tabulation considerably easier (keypunch, keyline, online data entry).

The principal advantage of graphic, adjectival, and numerical scales is their simplicity. The principal disadvantage is that, especially when many scales are laid out in a grid, they can be quite susceptible to some of the rater errors discussed in chapter 10, especially to central tendency.

Three variants of these scales deserve attention. Gagné and associates (for example, Gagné and Allaire 1974) constructed a dual reality/satisfaction scale such that respondents answer two questions about each instructor or course characteristic; for example (translated from the French):

A. How would you rate this instructor's clarity of language?

1	2	3	4	5
Never a Problem	Rarely a Problem	Occasionally a Problem	Frequently a Problem	Very Frequently a Problem

B. What rating on this item would you consider satisfactory?

1	2	3	4	5
Never a Problem	Rarely a Problem	Occasionally a Problem	Frequently a Problem	Very Frequently a Problem

The purpose of the second question is to build into the rating a norm or standard against which to interpret the response to the first question. The procedure is theoretically attractive (see the notion of threshold, chapter 7), and preliminary studies indicate reliability comparable to traditional rating formats (Levinthal, Lansky, and Andrews 1971; Gagné and Allaire, 1974). The frequency-of-problem labels also seem especially consistent with evaluation for diagnostic purposes.

Doyle (1975, p. 24) describes a dual evaluation/importance scale, which might take the following form:

A. How would you rate this instructor's openness to other points of view?

1	2	3	4	5
Poor	Fair	Good	Very Good	Excellent

B. How important is this instructor trait to you?

1	2	3
Not Very Important	Fairly Important	Very Important

In this case the second question is intended to furnish a way to distinguish the importance of the various questions on the questionnaire. Indeed, Crittenden and Norr (1974) found that specific-trait ratings weighted by item importance are better predictors of overall evaluations than are unweighted ratings. In addition, the importance ratings may give instructors and review committees a convenient estimate of item validity in the course at hand. Little other information on this scale exists, but informal observation suggests that the evaluation scale and the importance scale should be fairly different in form from one another, to reduce the chances that raters will fail to distinguish the two tasks.

A final variant of the traditional adjectival scale is especially relevant to outcome ratings. Students might rate their learning gains either by completing a rating at the beginning of a course and a parallel rating at the end, by answering a dual before/after rating only at the end of the course, or by using a single rating of the following sort:

How would you rate your grasp of the course material now as compared to that on the first day of this course?

Very Much Worse Now	Much Worse Now	Slightly Worse Now	Slightly Better Now	Much Better Now	Very Much Better Now

These three outcome-rating formats are similar in that they are all directed at the same goal and include an essential time component. They are different in that the first approach requires two administrations of a question-naire, the second requires one administration of a dual questionnaire, and the third requires one administration of a single questionnaire with a built-in before/after distinction. The sparse information that is available (for example, Howard et al. 1979) suggests that the third format is not only the most convenient but also the most effective.

A number of very specific questions are often asked with regard to the construction of adjectival or numerical scales. First, how many scale points should be used? In general, the more points the scale contains, the finer will be the distinctions raters can make and the more reliable the ratings will be, although these increases in reliability diminish quite rapidly after about ten points. On the other hand, experience shows that raters often find more than six or so points difficult to deal with, or annoying, or amusing, especially when labeling each point requires strained phrasing; for example:

3	4	5	6	7
Fairly Good	Quite Good	Very Good	Very, Very Good	Excellent

The ideal solution would probably be to tailor the number of scale points to the raters so that raters capable of very fine distinctions have many points to work with, and those troubled by many points have fewer. A practical solution might be six or seven points with bidirectional scales:

Strongly Disagree	Moderately Disagree	Slightly Disagree	Slightly Agree	Moderately Agree	Strongly Agree
1	2	3	4	5	6

and five or six points with unidirectional scales:

1	2	3	4	5
Poor	Fair	Good	Very Good	Excellent

provided that the wording of the labels does not do violence to language. When scoring-machine restrictions limit one to five points, it may be desirable to cast the questions in unidirectional format. If that procedure is unsatisfactory, a bidirectional format may be employed, though probably with some slight loss in reliability.

Bidirectional scales are usually symmetrical in that they contain an equal number of favorable and unfavorable labels; but there is good reason to construct asymmetrical scales such that there are more favorable scale points than unfavorable ones. Because most faculty will probably be rated toward the favorable end of the scale (owing to selection, experience, and leniency error) and because differentiation among faculty is a principal goal of most evaluation procedures, it is desirable to provide the most scale points where there are the most faculty to be rated. The common five-point poor/excellent scale illustrates this asymmetry.

Related to symmetry and number of scale points is the question of a neutral midpoint:

Strongly Agree	Agree	Neutral	Disagree	Strongly Disagree

Although such midpoints are very common, there is good reason not to use them. First, rating scales are already prone to central-tendency error and neutral midpoints seem to draw ratings toward the middle of the scale and thus to exacerbate the error. In addition, it is probably rare that raters are truly neutral, and a neutral midpoint may simply encourage lazy, superficial evaluation. More desirable than the scale just presented may be a scale without a neutral midpoint but with finer gradations between the center points:

Strongly Agree	Moderately Agree	Slightly Agree	Slightly Disagree	Moderately Disagree	Strongly Disagree

The occasional practice of using "Does Not Apply" as a midpoint is entirely unacceptable because it breaks the continuity of the scale. Raters should instead strike out or skip inapplicable items; a "Not Applicable" box could be provided, but physically away from the evaluation scale.

Some researchers recommend interspersing negatively phrased items (was unclear; failed to provide feedback) among positively phrased ones, apparently to keep raters attentive and to try to reduce rater error. This practice, however, seems more likely to create problems than to resolve them. If a rater is moving rapidly through a questionnaire (as many raters seem to do), failure to note the switch to negative phrasing is likely to result in considerably more serious error than simple halo or central tendency. Moreover, there is some suggestion in the technical literature that negatively phrased items are less effective than positive ones (Wiener 1982).

A final decision in the construction of adjectival and numerical scales is the choice between absolute and relative scale labels. Relative labels are those that make reference to some comparison group:

Far Below Average	Below Average	About Average	Above Average	Far Above Average

and absolute labels are those that do not:

Poor	Fair	Good	Very Good	Excellent

Relative scales are appealing because they appear to have a built-in norm, but closer inspection reveals that this norm could be quite misleading, because different raters probably have quite different notions of what constitutes average. Less indefinite would be an absolute scale empirically normed against a known group. Furthermore, it is easy to build a threshold into an absolute scale:

Unsatisfactory	Marginal	Fairly Good	Very Good	Excellent

Behaviorally Anchored Rating Scales (Bars)

From time to time, attempts have been made to reduce some of the rater error associated with traditional graphic, adjectival, and numerical scales. Behaviorally anchored rating scales (Smith and Kendall 1963; Campbell et al. 1973) are constructed according to procedures aimed at reducing the ambiguity inherent in traditional scales and scale labels. First, people familiar with the phenomenon to be rated (for example, teaching) are asked to describe instances of effective and ineffective behavior, after the fashion of Flanagan's (1954) critical-incidents technique. The researchers then sort these descriptions into a relatively small number of content categories and name those categories. As a check on the categorization, another group of knowledgeable observers again allocates the descriptions to the named categories. This group then rates each description for the degree of effectiveness it represents in its assigned category. Descriptions that the raters can effectively sort and rate are then set into a vertical scale for each category, with the behavioral descriptions serving as the scale labels.[1] These labels are empirically positioned along the continuum in proportion to the rated degree of effectiveness each represents:

Availability

Holds seminars in his home.

Meets with students in the union as well as in his office.

Is willing to work with students outside regular office hours.

Is readily available during office hours.

> Reluctantly sets up the fewest possible office hours.
>
> Refuses to see students outside of class.

The principle underlying behaviorally anchored rating scales is that these more performance-oriented, more behaviorally precise scales will result in more reliable and valid data. Unfortunately, the literature to date is not entirely encouraging (Schwab, Henneman, and DeCotiis 1975; Borman and Vallon 1974). That is, BARS scaling only sometimes increases reliability and validity (seldom decreases them), is very dependent on the groups of people who do the initial rating and sorting, and requires a great deal of work.

Forced-Choice Scales

Forced-choice scaling, another effort to increase the reliability and validity of ratings, was quite heavily researched by business, education, and military personnel specialists during the 1940s and 1950s. One popular forced-choice format comprises four elements, all of which are equally attractive to raters but only two of which actually correlate with some criterion measure and are scored. The remaining two elements, because they do not empirically distinguish effective and ineffective performance, are disregarded:

_____ Friendly

_____ Stimulating

_____ Scholarly

_____ Expressive

The score is the total number of discriminating elements chosen by the raters. The idea behind forced-choice scaling is that raters will not be able to fake favorable or unfavorable ratings, because all choices are equally desirable but only certain ones, unknown to the rater, are valid and therefore scored. As previously noted, Sharon and Bartlett (1969) found forced-choice scales considerably more resistant to rater error than traditional scales, and Wherry (1952), in his exceedingly thorough comparison of several scale formats, found that only forced-choice ratings correlated significantly with a student-learning measure.

Nevertheless, the usual conclusion about forced-choice scales is that they are unacceptable to raters, who resent "sneaky" measurement techniques; useless in diagnostic evaluation because they produce only a single, summary score; and inordinately difficult to devise. Forced-choice scales have all but dropped from view.

However, a recent paper (Wiener, 1982) reveals that the principal reason forced-choice scaling was abandoned is that middle-level business managers and military officers deplored being unable to manipulate ratings to reward favord subordinates. Wiener also argues that slight changes in the forced-choice format can reduce rater resistance. In addition, Doyle (1975, p. 26) points out that forced-choice scales can be set up to provide diagnostic evaluations by providing clusters of items that correspond to the general dimensions of good teaching.

The potential usefulness of forced-choice scales in instructional evaluation, especially evaluation for faculty personnel decisions, seems to have been seriously underestimated. A contemporary reexamination of the merits of this procedure is clearly in order.

Variable-Item Ratings

One of the ramifications of the historical tension between nomothetics and idiographics (described in chapter 7) is a competition between standard, preprinted questionnaires, which imply that the same dimensions of teaching are important in all courses, and questionnaires that tailor their content to the course at hand. Goal-attainment scaling and the cafeteria system reflect the idiographic point of view.

Kiresuk and Sherman's (1968) goal-attainment scaling is a procedure that permits raters to determine which rating items will be used. Developed in the context of psychotherapy evaluation by patients, goal-attainment scaling begins by having the patient construct a list of major symptoms or problems and create a kind of behaviorally anchored rating scale for personal progress in each category of symptoms. At repeated points during therapy, at the conclusion, and six months afterwards, the patient rates his own progress; he also rates the importance of each category of symptoms. Progress ratings summed across all of a given therapist's patients become an index of that therapist's effectiveness.

In an educational context, each student could prepare a list of his or her course goals and create a scale for each category of goals. Individual progress ratings could be diagnostically useful for the students as well as the instructor, and the combined progress ratings from all students could be used as an overall index of accomplishment. More information about the reliability of these outcome ratings will have to be provided before goal-attainment scaling can be recommended for use in important personnel decisions, and the procedure for combining ratings of varying outcomes across different students will require closer examination. Moreover, the procedure is inherently encumbered by the problem of attributing responsibility for student progress to the instructor rather than to the students. At least for diagnostic purposes and possibly for personnel-decision purposes, however, goal-attainment scaling is intriguing for its emphasis on achievement and for its attempt to introduce idiographic methodology to evaluation.

Derry and associates (1974; see also Starry, Derry, and Wright 1973) devised a procedure that allows instructors to select from a catalogue of items those that seem most appropriate for any given course. Their cafeteria system also permits departments and the institution itself to specify small numbers of core items to appear, along with the instructor-selected items, on the questionnaires of all their faculty. The departmental and institutional core items are used to compare faculty and to avoid the problem that some faculty might choose items on which they are likely to receive less favorable ratings, while others, for personnel-decision purposes, select more favorable items.

Doyle and Wattawa (1977) describe a variant of the cafeteria system that uses as its institutional core two of the general, summary items described in chapter 5:

How would you rate this instructor's overall teaching ability?

How much have you learned as a result of this course?

A very inexpensive approximation of this system might consist simply of an answer grid (adjectival or numerical scales without items). Instructors could overprint their own questions on these answer sheets, or hand out separate question sheets, or even announce the questions in class. An item catalogue could help instructors choose well phrased items, and departmental as well as institutional core items could be preprinted on the answer sheets.

The departmental and institutional core items allow these questionnaires to serve any purpose served by more traditional, standard questionnaires. The instructor-selected items, to the extent that the instructor is forthright and perceptive enough to select items that truly describe the most important features of the course, may provide the most valid questionnaires available for course diagnosis and improvement.

Mixed Formats

Mixing scale types on the same questionnaire may allow one to take advantage of the desirable qualities of different formats and may also result in a questionnaire that is more interesting to the raters than a questionnaire composed exclusively of one kind of scale.

One common mix is to combine ratings and essays in the same questionnaire to take advantage of the communication possibilities of essays and the quantitative features of ratings. Usually an instrument of this sort consists of a majority of rating items with one or two essay questions at the end. Another possibility would be an essentially essay questionnaire with one or two summary ratings at the beginning or end. Yet another variation would be to mix essays and ratings throughout the questionnaire so that each rating item had a space for prose comment, elaboration, or suggestion. In these questionnaires, the rater normally does the rating first and then (if so inclined) adds some brief remarks. An interesting alternative might be to put the essay question first, asking the rater to respond in some detail and then to do the rating. It is possible that the mental processes that go into formulating the essay response might result in a more thoughtful rating response.

Wiener (1982) indicates that a particular mix of rating items makes forced-choice scales more attractive to raters. The format is simply the usual four-element forced-choice arrangement, but in addition to selecting two of the four elements the rater rates each chosen element on a numerical scale:

	Friendly	1 2 3 4 5
	Stimulating	1 2 3 4 5
	Scholarly	1 2 3 4 5
	Expressive	1 2 3 4 5

Space for essay responses could also be added, to enhance the diagnostic usefulness of this format.

The technology of the cafeteria system has only begun to be exploited. In addition to the usual course and instructor characteristics, the item pool could contain a variety of student-outcome ratings, student characteristics, and even essay items (for example, ICES 1977; Doyle and Wattawa 1977). Furthermore, it should not be too difficult to program the system to allow a choice of rating scales: not only usual adjectival and numerical scales, but also the dual reality/satisfaction, evaluation/importance, and, for outcome items, the before/after formats. Finally, instructors could even write a few items of their own, which could be entered online into the system and appear on the questionnaire along with items chosen from the item pool. As already indicated, the cafeteria core could consist of two or three summary questions, or, if the renascent promise of forced-choice scaling is confirmed, of a small number of forced-choice items.

Training Raters

Varying scale types may make questionnaires more interesting to raters. It may also permit greater flexibility in the content of questionnaires, because item phrasing would not be limited to what agrees semantically with a particular scale arrangement, but the principal motivation behind research on scale types has been to improve the reliability and validity of ratings.

Some authors (for instance, Borman 1978, 1979; Schwab, Henneman, and DeCotiis, 1975) have concluded that there is little to be gained from further attempts to refine scale formats or create new ones, rather that more attention needs to be given to teaching raters to avoid the common rater errors. With the possible exception of forced-choice scales, this conclusion may well be correct, and, correct or not, training raters would still be a worthwhile practice.

Training raters may be a difficult task, however. It seems unlikely that an instructor will take class time to discuss halo and leniency error with student raters. It is possible, though certainly not assured, that brief oral comments just before an evaluation, or written instructions on a questionnaire, might have some impact on student ratings. Training might be more readily accomplished for colleague ratings (and be especially valuable there owing to the generally lower reliability of colleague ratings). Some further research on simple and effective ways to train raters would be worthwhile, but the cost of such training would have to be measured against whatever increases in reliability such training provides.

Note

1. Commenting on some advantages of vertical scales, Guilford (1954, chapter 11) notes that it is perhaps unfortunate that horizontal scales have become the mode, that scaling emulates the yardstick rather than the thermometer.

16 Tests

Some thoughtful observers (for example, Milton 1982) have expressed strong reservations about the quality of typical classroom tests. The principal concerns, as always, are reliability and validity. To the extent that classroom tests are deficient in reliability and validity, they do a disservice to students, and their usefulness in instructional evaluation is diminished. However, there is a vast body of literature (for instance, Thorndike 1971) that shows that tests can be highly reliable and valid if proper steps are taken to assure these qualities. The purpose of this chapter is to survey traditional, less traditional, and newer forms of classroom testing with special emphasis on improving reliability and validity by matching testing procedures to the kinds of learning one is attempting to measure, and by writing good, clear test questions.

Traditional Forms

Objective Tests

Forms of objective-test items include true/false, matching, fill-in-the-blank, and multiple choice, all of which share an advantage of efficiency in that they can cover a large amount of material on even a relatively short test, and an advantage of objectivity in that they can be scored by an untrained assistant provided only with an answer key. Most of these types of items can also be scored by machine.

True/false, matching, and fill-in-the-blank items, however, are limited by the fact that the learning they can measure is almost exclusively at the lowest recall-of-fact level of the Bloom et al. (1956) cognitive taxonomy discussed in chapter 4. These items are generally unsuitable for measurement of higher-level outcomes.

Multiple-choice items, on the other hand, are also efficient and objective, and they are suitable for assessment of higher-level outcomes. Moreover, the somewhat greater work required to construct multiple-choice items tends to result in tests of generally higher quality than those composed principally of the more easily constructed objective-item types. The principal disadvantages of multiple-choice items are that they, like all objective items, cannot readily appraise the student's ability to supply answers or explanations, to express ideas, or to create new products.

Most faculty are familiar with the basic structure of these kinds of objective items, but a few less-known variations deserve special mention. One variant of the true/false format was developed to meet the objection that students can mark an item false for many reasons, some of which are trivial or even spurious. With this variant, the student is required to change all false items to true, usually by writing on an accompanying line a correct word to replace an underscored key word in the item:

T   F   *three*   Gaul is divided into four parts.

Thus the true/false and fill-in-the-blank formats are blended, and the student is required, for false items, not only to indicate that the statement is false, but also to show why it is false.

Another version of the true/false format allows measurement of a somewhat higher level of learning, syllogistic reasoning. In this case, the student circles two answers for each item: T of F for true or false and CT or CF for the converse is true or the converse is false:

Ⓣ F   CT Ⓒ🅕   1. All numismatists are collectors.

T Ⓕ   Ⓒ🅣 CF   2. All arachnids are spiders.

An interesting and increasingly popular form of the basic multiple-choice item is the so-called multiple multiple choice:

Which of the following pairs of states lie(s) south of the Mason-Dixon Line?

   I.   Delaware and Pennsylvania
   II. Maryland and Virginia
   III. Connecticut and Maryland
   IV. North Carolina and West Virginia

   1. I only
   2. II only
   3. II and III
   4. II and IV

Items of this sort can be quite resistant to guessing and can require very precise knowledge or reasoning on the part of the student, but they may be particularly vulnerable to the criticism that no credit is given for partial knowledge.

The general editorial criteria for good objective items are that the phrasing of the items and the directions be clear, that the item type be commensurate with the level of learning desired, and that one and only one alternative be unequivocally correct. In addition, Gronlund (1981), Mehrens and Lehmann 1978, and Wesman (1971) provide detailed guidelines for the construction of each kind of item and a fairly elaborate discussion of the advantages and disadvantages of each type.

Essay Tests

The advantage of essay items, whether they call for long or short responses, is that they can measure "such outcomes as the ability to recall, organize, and integrate ideas; the ability to express oneself in writing; and ability to supply rather than merely identify interpretations and applications of data" (Gronlund 1981, p. 222).

The principal disadvantages of essay questions are that scoring can be quite unreliable and extrordinarily time-consuming; the amount of material that can be covered is very restricted, and responses may be unduly affected by the student's verbal skills, penmanship, and capacity for blarney. Short-answer essay questions are probably less vulnerable to many of these problems than are long-answer questions, but sometimes it is the very freedom of the long-answer question that makes the essay form appropriate. Essay questions are not efficient measures of factual material, and, of course, the use of essay questions does not assure that what is being measured is truly higher-level learning.

The general editorial criteria for good essay questions are that they be used only when the intended learning cannot be satisfactorily measured by objective items and that the item clearly define the students's task.

Gronlund (1981), Mehrens and Lehmann (1978), and Coffman (1971) provide further guidelines and discussion.

Less Traditional Forms

The Interpretive Exercise

An interpretive exercise consists of a set of objective and/or essay questions focused on a common body of information: maps, charts, tables, pictures, prose, or poetry. The interpretive exercise can provide a very realistic measure of quite complex skills, especially problem-solving skills. Moreover, it standardizes the students' task by providing all students with the same circumscribed body of information from which to work, and it provides what many students may consider more engaging and stimulating testing. Its principal disadvantage is that it can be very difficult to con-struct. In addition, the interpretive exercise shares the advantages and disadvantages of the kinds of objective and essay items it incorporates.

Editorial criteria for the stimulus material (for instance, the map on which the questions are based) are that it be new to the students, reasonably brief, and pertinent to the intended learning in the course. In addition, all of the editorial criteria for the particular kinds of test items apply.

A wide variety of interpretive exercises is discussed in Gronlund (1981), Mehrens and Lehmann (1978) and Wesman (1971).

Specialized Forms

A number of item types have been developed to serve the special needs of particular disciplines. In foreign languages, for example, the cued-closes item is common (for example, Sweet 1968):

Arma *and a man* cano . . .

Virumque—I sing of arms and a man . . . *[Aeneid]*

Here the student translates the basic statement from Latin to English and also translates the English phrase in the basic statement to Latin. The advantage of this kind of item over simple translation is that it can require a considerable degree of precision of the student. The disadvantage is that, like any translation item, its scoring involves a degree of subjectivity and hence unreliability.

In English composition or in foreign languages, the interlinear exercise blends the controlled-stimulus quality of multiple-choice tests with the freedom of expression of essay tests. Presented with a sample of deficient writing, the student identifies the deficiencies and corrects them:

　　　　　hold　　　　　　　　*to be*
We think that these truths are self-evident . . .

Such items can measure higher order skills such as evaluation, but can also be rather difficult to score.

Newer Developments

Three new avenues of research in classroom testing deserve attention: partial-credit scoring, simulation exercises, and adaptive testing. Partial-credit scoring was conceived as a means to make more complete use of information that may be contained in a test, hence to achieve more valid measurement of learning. In many tests, one of the incorrect alternatives may be more nearly correct than the others; the student choosing it shows more grasp of the material than do students choosing the other incorrect alternatives—but less grasp than those choosing the correct alternative. Partial-credit scoring attempts to give some credit for that partial grasp. One avenue to giving partial credit is simply for the instructor to decide which, if any, incorrect alternatives selected deserve partial credit, and to assign some fraction of a point to the student's score for the choice of that alternative. Another route is to have the students rate their confidence in the correctness of each response they give, and then to give most credit for correct scores in which students indicate highest confidence, less credit for different combinations of correct and incorrect scores and greater and lesser confidence. The advantages to partial-credit scoring procedures are that they use more information than do traditional scoring procedures, and that some variations (for example, the student-confidence ratings) may provide additional useful feedback for course improvement purposes. Unfortunately, partial-credit procedures rarely improve the validity of test scores and frequently add considerably to the difficulty of scoring. In short, they do not often seem to be very cost effective. Weiss and Davison (1981) provide a detailed review of partial-credit scoring methods.

Simulation exercises attempt to approximate real-life tasks especially of the diagnostic, problem-solving variety. For example, a medical student might be presented with initial information about a patient and be asked to make a step-by-step diagnosis. A variety of medical procedures, laboratory tests, and other sources of information are named on a special answer sheet or computer screen, and the student is to choose, one at a time, those that would result in an efficient and accurate diagnosis. Each choice of a source gives the student additional information that may influence his choice of the next source. The student's score is a function of both the number of sources chosen (the fewer the better, to keep patient cost to a minimum) and the sequence in which he chooses them (the extent to which his sequence approximates an ideal sequence determined by experts in the field). The advantage of these simulation exercises is their ability to measure realistic, highly complex behavior under controlled conditions. Their disadvantage is their considerable difficulty of construction. The importance of diagnostic training especially in some professional schools may well make these procedures worth that effort, however. McGuire and Babbott (1967) describe the construction and application of these exercises in medical schools, Burris et al. (1979) in law schools.

Adaptive testing is the name for a variety of testing procedures aimed at increasing the precision and efficiency of testing by tailoring the difficulty of the items to each particular student's level of achievement. In one version of adaptive testing, the student answers a small number of questions of widely varying difficulty, and the responses are used to identify a level of difficulty for more intensive testing. With this procedure, a smaller net number of items can be used, and those that are used can more accurately locate the student's level of achievement. Adaptive testing is often done with computers, sometimes with special answer sheets. The principal advantages of adaptive testing are its efficiency and precision, the principal disadvantage—as with most of the less traditional forms of testing—its complexity of construction. Weiss (forthcoming) reviews many varieties of adaptive testing procedures.

Within the limitations described in Chapters 2 and 7, tests can be useful instruments for course diagnosis and improvement. The more carefully traditional objective and essay items are constructed, the more useful and defensible they are likely to be.[1] When circumstances warrant their use, the more specialized and some of the newer forms of testing can also result in more reliable and valid information about the course and the instructor.

Note

1. Construction and evaluation of a test should include not only the editorial considerations discussed in this chapter, but also a test plan and item- and test-analysis statistics.

Part V:
Applications

17 Collecting and Reporting Data

It is regrettable that less attention is generally given to the actual collection of evaluations than to the instruments on which they are collected, and still less is given to the ways evaluative data are reported. Chapter 12 concluded that the circumstances surrounding an evaluation, especially the social context, may have a significant effect on the data, and surely the form in which information is reported may influence how it is interpreted and may even determine whether it is used.

Chapter 12 also provided some guidance on those conditions that are most likely to influence evaluations, and proposed that some degree of standardization of conditions is desirable, particularly with respect to the stated purposes of the evaluation, the proximity to psychologically significant events as examinations and holidays, the choice and demeanor of the person who administers the evaluation, and the instructor's access to the data before tabulation. Less information exists on the technical features of report formats that may affect evaluations, but it seems reasonable to propose that the qualities of good report formats parallel the qualities of good reading materials, which in turn parallel the qualities of a good instructor, because a data report is no less instructional in nature than a course handout, a test, or a lecture. The qualities of good report formats, then, are that they be technically sound, clear, palatable, and even engaging. Moreover, data reports may be more effective when they are tailored to their particular audiences. Beyond these general guidelines, the specific features of a data report, as well as the degree and kind of standardization of conditions that is desirable, depend largely on the purpose of the evaluation.

Course Diagnosis and Improvement

Data intended for use in course diagnosis and improvement need to be collected in such a way that they communicate the evaluators' perceptions with reasonable accuracy and considerable thoroughness, and to be reported in such a way that instructors can and will use them to help understand the specific strengths and weaknesses in their courses and act upon any deficiencies.

Diagnostic evaluations are relatively informal, and they may be performed early on in the course and quite frequently thereafter. If standardization in the collection of evaluations means the use of a proctor and a special script to administer the evaluation, requirements that evaluation conditions be standardized will not encourage diagnostic evaluations. If standardization requires that evaluations be administered at a particular time in the term, it may even discourage evaluation. On the other hand, the absence of standardization of these kinds may introduce some bias. An acceptable resolution of this problem may be to encourage faculty to perform their own informal diagnostic evaluations whenever and as often as they please, to educate them about the possible influences of lack of standardization on their evaluation, and either to exclude those evaluations from personnel decisions or to require that they be accompanied by a statement of who administered the evaluation, when, for what stated purpose, under what circumstances, and whether or not the instructor had had access to the data before they were tabulated. Exluding these data from personnel decisions or requiring this special statement about the conditions surrounding the evaluation protects both the instructor and the system; for example, the instructor may be disadvantaged if evaluators believe the data are for private course-improvement purposes, and the system may be weakened if some instructors are able to improve their evaluations by their behavior just before or during the evaluation. Because the most helpful diagnostic evaluations probably come from conversations and essay evaluations, which are of limited usefulness in administrative evaluation, excluding these from administrative use is not likely to impede the personnel-decision process.

Evaluative conversations and essay questionnaires do not really produce evaluation reports in the way that computer tabulations of ratings do, but an instructor can, alone or in conjunction with a mentor or consultant, prepare his or her own report or summary of the data. The instructor might, for example, read and summarize in writing all of the responses to the first item, then do the same for each subsequent question one at a time. These summaries, along with any overall comments, confirmations, or rebuttals the instructor elects to give (and the statement describing the conditions surrounding the evaluation) would become a record that the instructor could study, alone or with a consultant, in preparation for the next offering of that course. This technique could be even more beneficial if the instructor were to do an explicit self-evaluation before examining the student or peer reports. Centra (1973) has shown that instructors whose self-evaluations are significantly more favorable than their student evaluations are the most likely to improve their teaching. The self-evaluation could be either real or ideal, that is, based on how the instructor really is or on how he would like to be.

The utility of this procedure is not just in the written report. Of at least equal value for course-improvement purposes is the very act of preparing a record in this fashion, for the greater concentration required to study, summarize, and respond to evaluations should lead to a deeper understanding of the course. Including in that written record specific plans of course improvement—for instance, one particular problem to be worked on, one new tack to take next time, or, conceivably, a detailed revision of the entire course—should lead to an even more useful evaluation.

Any evaluation summarized along these lines, but especially a student evaluation done quite early in the course, could provide the basis for constructive in-class discussion during which the instructor could present his summary of the data, ask for clarification and elaboration, and present his own point of view and plans for the future. The diagnostic and even pedagogical value of this sort of dialogue may outweigh the loss of instructional time and the initial anxiety that dialogue entails. Some instructors approximate this procedure by distributing to their students mimeographed copies of the evaluation summary and plan for the future, an approach that saves time but sacrifices the advantages of dialogue with students.

Diagnostic evaluations can also be collected in the form of ratings, usually ratings by students. Adjectival or numerical rating scales are adequate for diagnostic evaluations; the more rigorous scaling methods (see chapter 15) are probably not cost effective for this purpose. The quantitative features of ratings can lead to any of a variety of report formats. The most basic format for reporting ratings consists of tables of summary statistics such as means, standard deviations, and frequency distributions. The mean is the arithmetic average, an indication of what the typical student said. The standard deviation is a measure of agreement among raters; the lower the standard deviation the more agreement there was and the more precisely the mean represents the opinion of the whole group. A frequency distribution is a tabulation of the numbers of percentages of raters who chose each point on the scale; it is perhaps the best statistic for conveying the range and spread of a set of evaluations.

There is some controversy about the use of medians versus means. The median is the midpoint in a serial arrangement of individual ratings. It differs from the mean in that the median is less influenced by extremely favorable or unfavorable responses. One's choice between mean and median thus depends in part on how much emphasis one wants to place on extreme scores. The choice is further influenced by certain technical properties of the rating scale (equal intervals, see Siegel 1956), but because the goal of evaluation of this sort is to provide only a general indication of instructional quality, (for instance, unsatisfactory, satisfactory, outstanding) and because on a typical five- to seven-point scale there is not likely to be a great deal of difference between the median and the mean, it does not seem terribly important which statistic is used (Baker, Hardyk, and Petronovick

1966) so long, of course, that one does not compare one instructor's mean to another's median. It may be worth presenting both medians and means, to reduce some of the complaint that inevitably comes from the exclusive use of one or the other. (Technically, the semi-interquantile range is the median's analogue to the standard deviation, but that and other interquartile statistics are exceedingly rare.)

More elaborate data reports involve some kind of norm or comparison group. Norms may be expressed in percentile terms, that is, the instructor's rank in an ordering of instructors; or as deviation scores, in which ratings are reported in terms of standard deviations from the mean of a comparison group; or in more complicated but intriguing ways (see Gronlund 1981, pp. 387–391).

More problematical than the statistics of norms is the selection of the group of instructors or courses that comprises the comparison group. The too-common practice of presenting a norm based on the ratings of, say, all associate professors in an institution seems more misleading than enlightening, because, for example, such a norm treats as comparable the introductory lecture course and the senior seminar. It also treats as comparable students in different disciplines who probably (Centra 1973) have quite different instructional needs and standards for good teaching and course material that may be differentially difficult to teach. A more defensible set of norms would be based on comparable courses—courses in which the instructors are trying to teach the same kind of material to the same kinds of students under the same kinds of conditions. Thus the categorizing variables would include verbal versus numerical course content (Anastasi 1976, p. 184); lower- versus higher-level instructional goals; beginning, intermediate, or advanced content; student type (chapter 6); and class size. Moreover, the norm group should consist either of all courses in the institution (or unit) or a random sample of those courses, perhaps stratified by level and term, as distinguished from some undefined collection of courses in which the instructors simply happened to have used the same questionnaire. A reasonable alternative in large departments would be to avoid the difficulties of institutional norms and use only the courses in that department, sorted into comparable groups. Two or three moderate-size departments might even pool data for a common norm group, provided that the material, students, and teaching conditions are reasonably comparable.

Some evaluation services supply regional or even national norms. These norms appear interesting in that local faculty (and administrators) may be able to get from them some idea of how their teaching compares to teaching elsewhere, but such information is of limited value and certainly does not outweigh the requirement that courses in the norm group be comparable in terms of content, teaching conditions, and students. Indeed, the broader the norm group the less likely it is that this requirement of comparability will have been met.

Easy to lose sight of is the importance of ipsative and mastery interpretations, which complement, and, in evaluation for course diagnosis and
improvement, may be more useful than, normative interpretations. Ipsative
interpretation is the examination of one's own strengths and weaknesses
without reference to any external standard, in effect the listing of an
instructor's item ratings from most to least favorable. In ipsative interpretation, the most favorable ratings reinforce desirable traits and behaviors, the
least favorable suggest change. Mastery, or absolute (Doyle 1975, p. 97)
interpretation means choosing a threshold level of quality below which the
rating will be considered unacceptable, much like a cut-off score on a
driver's license examination. This threshold score is partly a function of the
wording of the rating scale (that is, a rating of *good* means good) and partly
of one's prior experience with evaluations. Thus there is an interplay among
the three principal modes of data comparison: normative data guide the
selection of a threshold for mastery interpretation, and mastery thresholds
indicate the point below which ratings are unacceptable in ipsative interpretation.

A refined evaluation program for instructional diagnosis and improvement would also provide for cross-tabulation, especially of student ratings.
Cross-tabulation is the tabulation of data from groups of raters independently, the tabulation, for example, of ratings from female students and
male students separately. Cross-tabulation enables one to see if an instructor is more effective with some kinds of students than with others. The principle of cross-tabulation is a simple and appealing one; the difficulties are
determining which rater characteristics to use as the sorting variables and
how to measure some of them. Chapters 6 and 12 suggested some important
student and peer characteristics, but concluded that the gains from cross-
tabulation are generally modest at best. Until research into rater and ratee
interactions is more advanced, and more convenient measures are devised,
instructors or departments should probably rely on their own best judgment
of which characteristics are worth using as categorization variables. Alter-
natively, evaluation questionnaires could contain questions about a variety
of rater characteristics; actual correlations between ratings and these characteristics could be routinely computed and cross-tabulations prepared for
those characteristics that correlate significantly with evaluations.

Evaluative data, especially normative data, and especially when cross-
tabulated, are most often presented in tabular form, but the reports may be
clearer, more palatable, and even more engaging if the reports are tailored
to different kinds of faculty. Although there seems to be little if any
research to support this notion, it may be that faculty in some disciplines are
more used to working with tables of numbers and more adept at interpret-
ing them, while other faculty work better with prose, and still others with
graphic presentations such as pie charts and bar graphs. Doyle and Bejar
(1973) proposed a computer-based data reporting plan in which ratings

would be translated to prose. Different mean ratings and standard deviations would cause the program to print out different interpretive paragraphs. Especially high ratings would result in compliments, and ratings below a threshold would produce specific suggestions for improving the course, along with references to relevant books, articles, and services. It would also be possible to offer faculty the choice of tabular, prose, or graphic reports, or always to provide tables and offer prose and graphs as optional additional services, perhaps for the same kind of modest fee one often encounters for item analysis of classroom examinations. An instructor's guide to evaluation, a simple and inexpensive booklet, could provide much the same kind of course-improvement information, though not tailored to individual sets of data. A nice complement to either the computer-based system or the instructor's guide would be a selection of good books kept conveniently accessible in departments, libraries, or the faculty lounge.

Student performances on classroom tests can also be used in course diagnosis and improvement. Basic information would come from comparing the average examination score of the course at hand to the averages of previous classes, assuming that test difficulty and student ability and motivation have not changed. More complete information could come from an item-by-item inspection of the test, with an eye toward those topics with which students are having greatest difficulty (ipsative interpretation), and those on which student performance falls below that of previous classes (normative interpretation), or below the instructor's expectations (mastery interpretation). Sharing this information with the class could also be a very useful practice, perhaps helping to determine how much strong or weak learning is due to the instructor and how much to the students.

Finally, there is a significant body of literature that indicates that evaluative data are more likely to contribute to instructional improvement when those data are communicated to the instructor by a respected consultant or master teacher (Pambookian 1973, Aleamoni 1974; see also Doyle 1975, pp. 83–84). Similarly, experience indicates that the most effective instructional-improvement programs are those that employ individual or small-group consultation over a long period of time (for example, Parker and Lawson 1978). Such intensive consultation programs, however, can be quite expensive and can reach relatively few faculty. On the other hand, participating faculty have reported that the experience was worth the expense (Ullian and Parker 1980), and former participants may become consultants to their colleagues, thus increasing exponentially the number of faculty served. If these consultation services are as effective as the data so far suggest, they would be very constructive complements to evaluation reports, and they should force faculty and administrators to make some very difficult decisions about institutional priorities and expenditures.

Grasha (1977), Centra (1979), Seldin (1980), and Millman (1981) describe in detail a variety of procedures for using student, colleague, and self-evaluations, as well as student achievement, in evaluation for course diagnosis and improvement.

Personnel Decisions

Evaluative data intended for use in personnel decisions need to be collected in such a way that error is minimized and presented in such a way that review committees and administrators will use them properly, and in proportion to their rigor.

The problem of standardization is acute in personnel evaluation, not only because ethics requires fairness in the collection and interpretation of data, but also because of the legal implications of any significant weaknesses in the evaluation program. Lawyers can be expected to pay a great deal of attention to any factors that might make evaluations spuriously more or less favorable. Of special interest to the institution's attorney defending a personnel decision would be any factor that might have led to unduly high ratings, especially any opportunity for an instructor to tamper with the data or to exert social influence on the raters. Of similar interest to the claimant's lawyer would be any factor that might have depressed the ratings, such as the unqualified use in personnel decisions of evaluations collected explicitly for private course-improvement purposes.

The best way to avoid problems of this sort might be to devise a rigorous standardization program for personnel evaluation and to exclude from the administrative process any data not collected under these standardized conditions. As a minimum, standardization would require either that instructors follow a common script in the administration of evaluations or that special proctors (or students in the class) distribute and collect the questionnaires, that the script (or the questionnaire or both) clearly indicate that the data may be used in important personnel decisions, and that the instructor have absolutely no access to the evaluations before they are sent in for processing. The problem is that such rigid practices are a nuisance and distasteful to many faculty and students, so policies requiring standardization are likely to be disregarded in some institutions. Faculty, administrators, and students will just have to choose between the annoyance of a standardized evaluation procedure and the very real possibility that evaluations will be seriously weakened in the most difficult decisions by the absence of standardization.

Given some acceptable degree of standardization, the most valid and defensible data for use in personnel evaluations are those that come from summary-rating items, although some specific ratings may be used if the faculty can provide a strong enough argument for the validity of these ratings in particular courses, and essay evaluations may be used if they are scored by at least a few qualified readers. Adjectival and numerical scales are probably adequate for personnel data, but, as noted in chapter 15, forced-choice scaling may develop into the method of choice. Means (or medians) and standard deviations are the most appropriate statistics for reporting personnel ratings, because computing averages cancels out a certain amount of error and produces a more reliable statistic. Frequency distributions may, however, be used in addition, to present the data in more detail and to illustrate variability. Both normative and mastery interpretations may be employed, the former to provide an external standard when other faculty are trying to teach the same kind of material to the same kinds of students under similar circumstances, the latter to indicate levels below which the ratings are unsatisfactory and above which they are outstanding. Ipsative interpretation is not useful in personnel evaluation. Either tabular or graphic presentations, or both, are acceptable, depending on the audience at hand; but computer-generated prose interpretations may involve too many arbitrary decisions (for instance, cut-off points) for administrative use. Finally, cross-tabulation is appropriate in personnel evaluation whenever there is reason to believe that the instructor is differentially effective with various kinds of students.

Although self-evaluations probably have little if any place in personnel evaluations, certain kinds of information from the instructor could add to the meaningfulness of the overall evaluation. As previously noted, the instructor could point out any departures from standardization that might have influenced the data. In addition, the instructor should point out any special circumstances that might bear on the evaluation—a promising new teaching method that failed, an especially difficult group of students—and express any reservations about the dependability of the evaluation. There may be some advantage to asking all instructors to address these issues to keep the kinds of available information constant and so that the instructor who does express reservation is not automatically characterized as defensive or unable to take criticism.

In a similar vein, informal observation suggests that personnel evaluations may be as much influenced by the form in which data are presented as by the substance of those data. Thus faculty with refined writing and data skills may have an advantage over their colleagues in ways that may have little to do with instructional effectiveness, and inexperienced faculty, or faculty new to an institution, may be at a disadvantage in comparison to their more experienced colleagues. To reduce these possible inequities, and to simplify and expedite review-committee deliberations, departments or divisions might describe a model personnel portfolio that instructors could approximate in content and in form.

Among the principal consumers of personnel ratings are faculty review committees and departmental and divisional administrators. Because of the important roles they play in personnel decisions, and because of the increasingly litigious nature of personnel administration, it is imperative that these people receive at least basic instruction in the psychometrics of evaluation and the legal implications of their procedures. A personnel decisions handbook may be one route to this instruction. Such a handbook could contain, in addition to a description of the model portfolio just proposed, a set of guidelines for the use of data in faculty personnel decisions; for example, the minimum numbers of students and classes, and of peer observers of classroom teaching and course materials, required to provide an adequate body of data; the advantages and disadvantages of student, peer, and self-evaluations, and classroom tests, in the appraisal of the scholarly foundation of a course, the presentation, and the outcomes; a list of factors that might affect student, peer, and self evaluations; instructions on the desirability of summary-rating items and about those kinds of arguments that might possibly justify the use of other items; guidelines on normative and mastery interpretations; caveats on common misuses of data such as over-interpretation of small differences, leniency error on the part of raters and review committee members, and the tendency to let isolated experiences and interesting anecdotes overpower systematically collected data; explanation of the summary statistics that appear in the report; and a thorough description of any norms that may be available. The handbook could also contain some description of the legal requirements and consequences of personnel decisions; for example, the obligations borne by the institution with respect to equal opportunity and affirmative action, especially with regard to the rigorous validation some courts may require of evaluation procedures that, on their face, seem to have an adverse impact on protected classes of people; the importance of adhering scrupulously to any institutional policies on personnel evaluation (procedural due process); other constitutional rights on which evaluation may not infringe (for instance, free speech); and liabilities of review committee members as well as any defense and indemnification guaranteed by the institution. Indeed, the legal requirements for personnel evaluation are growing complex enough—and the consequences of violations expensive enough—that personnel-evaluation policies ought to be reviewed by counsel before they are promulgated, and a responsible and knowledgeable individual ought to be charged with monitoring compliance. General information on the legal aspects of personnel evaluation is presented in Kaplan (1978), Cascio (1978, chapter 2), and Centra (1979, chapter 7). More specific information should, of course, be sought from local counsel. Finally, Centra (1979), Seldin (1980), and Millman (1981) also address the roles of student, colleague, and self-evaluation, and student achievement in evaluation for personnel decisions.

Advising and Course Selection

The principal audiences for data for advising and course-selection purposes are students and their academic advisors. Hence the data should be in such a form that these people can and will use them to choose courses that will be most beneficial to the students, both in content and in presentation. The data, standardization, and report formats most appropriate for this purpose of evaluation are not much different from those for personnel decisions: summary ratings collected under rather consistent conditions, reported in statistical fashion with mastery or normative interpretation, and perhaps cross-tabulated by important student characteristics. Some faculty and administrators experienced in this form of evaluation recommend the use of summary statistics such as means, medians, and standard deviations, while others recommend frequency distributions; some prefer tabular presentation while others prefer graphic or prose formats. The proponents of summary statistics argue that means and standard deviations are easier to use than frequency distributions and take less space in publications. The advocates of frequency distributions argue that the problem of large standard errors of means in small classes is too difficult to deal with when evaluation results are so widely distributed, and that summary statistics make comparisons among noncomparable courses too easy. The proponents of summary statistics seem to have the stronger argument, provided the ultimate publication clearly defines the statistics and emphasizes the dangers of evaluation in small classes and the noncomparable nature of many sets of courses. (It follows that mastery interpretation may be more desirable in this context than normative interpretation unless separate norms are provided and students and advisors are clearly instructed how to use them.) Advocates of tabular formats contend that tables of numbers are the most efficient way to communicate data, but proponents of graphic and prose formats argue that their methods are easier for students to understand. Effectiveness seems a stronger argument than efficiency, so the somewhat greater cost (in terms of development, scoring, and space in a publication) of the graphic and prose formats may be justified. Graphic or prose formats, however, seem incomplete without numbers, so a sensible solution may be to pick one or perhaps as many as two items (for example, overall course effectiveness, overall teaching ability), print out their means and standard deviations, and translate each mean through normative or mastery interpretation into, say, a five-star system (as in the travel and dining guides) or into computer-generated words (poor, fair, good, and so forth; or below average, about average, above average, and so forth). Such translations, however, are only as good as the decision rules in the computer program and will always be—as any grading system—vulnerable to charges of arbitrariness.

Quality of teaching, however, is only one of a number of reasons for choosing courses. To avoid overemphasizing evaluations, the Student Course Information Project at the University of Minnesota, publishes a course guide containing detailed course descriptions furnished by instructors, essays on course selection and program planning written by a psychologist, and summary evaluation ratings supplied by students. The course descriptions (see figure 17–1) include such information as nature and type of exams, amount of reading, cost of books, and course emphasis (in terms of Bloom's taxonomy), nature of class sessions (lecture, demonstration, recitation) and so on. The essays on course selection and program planning emphasize perspective by pointing out the importance of sampling a variety of courses to test one's interest, choosing courses that complement tentative career goals, and seeking courses that meet or enlarge on the students' academic abilities and educational needs, as well as selecting instructors that appear to be especially good teachers.

A Unified Program

Although there are sharp differences among evaluation programs intended for course diagnosis and improvement, personnel decisions, and student course selection, it is entirely possible for a single system—even a single questionnaire—to serve all three purposes.

In a unified program, the basic student evaluation questionnaire (figure 17–2) might consist of four parts: two or three summary rating items, eight or ten specific rating items that deal with traits and behaviors that are important in many courses, a few questions about student characteristics, and space for up to ten or so items that instructors choose from a catalogue of essay or rating questions. The summary items would be used for personnel purposes and course selection; the instructor's own essay or rating items would be for course diagnosis and improvement; the specific ratings would be for diagnostic use in very large courses or courses in which the instructor prefers not to use the item catalogue; and the questions about student characteristics would be for cross-tabulation. The same questionnaire could be used in self or peer evaluation, especially if a few questions about the scholarly foundation of the course were added. These questionnaires could be preprinted, or they could be entirely prepared by computer in cafeteria fashion.

The questionnaires, item catalogues, instructor's guides, and personnel-decisions handbooks could be obtained from the evaluation office, bookstore, or other repository, and the data (except essay evaluations) could be tabulated (and, when desirable, cross-tabulated) by the evaluation office, computer center, other support unit, or even an outside vendor.

Course (*e.g., GER 1-001*): _____ Section(s): _____ Instructor: _____

Course Title: _____

PURPOSE OF COURSE:

INTENDED STUDENT AUDIENCE:
(Rank in priority order, 1 = first priority)

___ Dept. majors/pre-majors/minors

___ Majors in related fields

___ Other students, for general education

___ Other: _____

COST OF REQUIRED MATERIALS, TEXT(S):

About $ _____

METHODS OF INSTRUCTION

INSTRUCTION TIME-Scheduled hours per week

___ Lecture

___ Demonstration

___ Lecture/demonstration via closed-circuit TV or film

___ Recitation/discussion

___ Lab

COURSE EMPHASIS-Percent on each:

___ % Basic knowledge and principles

___ % Application of knowledge/principles

___ % Analysis, synthesis, evaluation

___ % Skill, manipulation, practice

___ % Attitudes, values, self-awareness

___ % Other: _____

INSTRUCTIONAL AIDS Used Extensively:
(check as many as apply)

[ ] Demonstrations

[ ] Films, slides, prints, etc.

[ ] Closed-circuit TV

[ ] Computers

[ ] Guest Lecturers

[ ] Other: _____

OUT-OF-CLASS LEARNING ACTIVITIES

EXAMINATIONS

NUMBER of Exams

___ Final Exam

___ Mid-quarter exam(s)

___ Quizzes

TYPE of Final and Mid-Quarter Exams:
(check as many as apply)

[ ] Closed-book

[ ] Open-book

[ ] Take-home

[ ] Oral

[ ] Presentation or performance

[ ] Other: _____

FORMAT of Exam Questions:

[ ] Multiple-option, true-false

[ ] Short answer, fill-in-the-blank

___ Student presentations
___ Individual student conferences

CLASS SIZE-Number for each:
___ Lecture/demonstration/discussion
___ Recitation/discussion section
___ Lab section

RESPONSIBILITY OF TAs, if any:
(check as many as apply)
[ ] No TA
[ ] Full course
[ ] Lecture
[ ] Recitation/discussion section
[ ] Lab section
[ ] Individual student conferences
[ ] Correcting papers, reports, exams
[ ] Assigning grades
[ ] Extra help (e.g., office hours)
[ ] Other:___

REQUIRED READING:
___ Pages-Textbooks
___ Pages-Library materials
        (books, articles)

REQUIRED PAPERS AND REPORTS
(number of each)
___ Major research reports/term papers
___ Brief written reports or papers
___ Oral reports
___ Problem-solving assignments
___ Special projects (e.g., field work)
___ Computer assignments

EXPECTED out-of-class EFFORT:
___ Hours per week

EXTRA HELP available-Hours per week
___ Scheduled (e.g., office hours)
___ Available for unscheduled extra help

[ ] Short essay
[ ] Long essay
[ ] Problems
[ ] Other:___

GRADING

BASIS OF GRADE-Percent of final grade
___% Final exam
___% Mid-quarter exam(s)
___% Quizzes
___% Lab activities or reports
___% Problem-solving assignments
___% Written reports or papers
___% Class presentation/performance
___% Class participation
___% Other: please specify___

Figure 17-1. Questionnaire for Collecting Course Descriptions

STUDENT OPINION SURVEY

This questionnaire provides the opportunity for you to express your opinions about the teaching in this course. Your evaluation will go to the instructor for use in improving the course; specified parts of it may also go to the administration for use in important personnel decisions about your instructor and for publication in a course guide to help students choose courses. Please be thoughtful and candid. Thanks for your help.

I. Your answers to these first five questions will help determine how well this instructor is reaching different kinds of students.

1. In which year in school are you?

Freshman	Sophomore	Junior	Senior	Graduate Student
1	2	3	4	5

2. Which of the following best describes your typical grades?

Almost All As	Mostly As and Bs	Mostly Bs and Cs	Mostly Cs or Lower
1	2	3	4

3. What grade do your expect to receive in this course?

Lower than I Usually Get	About the Same As I Usually Get	Higher than I Usually Get
1	2	3

4. Please rank the following statements as to how well they describe you: (1 = Best description, 2 = Next best, etc.)

____ I enjoy school; I'm persistent and want to do my best.

____ I find school boring, futile; I prefer to be by myself.

____ I'm very energetic, a "driver"; I enjoy pressure.

____ I hate pressure; I try to avoid confrontation.

5. To what extent have you felt "on the same wave length" with your instructor?

Very Little	Little	Some	Much	Very Much	Extremely Much
1	2	3	4	5	6

II. Your answers to these questions will be especially useful in the improvement of teaching in this course. Please circle one answer for each item.

	Unsatisfactory	Marginal	Good	Very Good	Excellent
1. This instructor's effectiveness in helping you distinguish what's important from what's not.	1	2	3	4	5
2. . . . helping keep you interested in learning.	1	2	3	4	5
3. . . . keeping you aware of course goals.	1	2	3	4	5
4. . . . presenting the subject matter.	1	2	3	4	5
5. . . . providing helpful feedback.	1	2	3	4	5
6. . . . helping you hold on to what you've learned.	1	2	3	4	5
7. . . . keeping you challenged.	1	2	3	4	5
8. . . . maintaining rapport with students.	1	2	3	4	5
9. . . . trying to reach all the different kinds of students in this course.	1	2	3	4	5

Source: © University of Minnesota Measurement Services Center. Reproduced with Permission.

Figure 17-2. Outline of a Questionnaire for a Unified Instructional-Evaluation Program

Figure 17–2 continued

III. Your answers to these next three questions may be used in important salary and promotion decisions about this instructor. They may also be published in a course guide to help students choose courses.

1. How would you rate this instructor's overall teaching in this course?

Unsatisfactory 1	Marginal 2	Good 3	Very Good 4	Excellent 5

2. How would you rate the overall quality of this course?

Unsatisfactory 1	Marginal 2	Good 3	Very Good 4	Excellent 5

3. How much have you learned as a result of this course?

Little 1	Some 2	Much 3	Very Much 4	A Very Great Amount 5

IV. Your instructor may supply some additional questions. Please answer them here or on a separate sheet, as your instructor indicates.

1.	1	2	3	4	5	6
2.	1	2	3	4	5	6
3.	1	2	3	4	5	6
4.	1	2	3	4	5	6
5.	1	2	3	4	5	6

6.	1	2	3	4	5	6
7.	1	2	3	4	5	6
8.	1	2	3	4	5	6
9.	1	2	3	4	5	6
10.	1	2	3	4	5	6

The instructor would receive tabulations of all rating items and could direct that tabulations only of the summary ratings go to the department chair or the advising office. Norms for student ratings on the summary items (and perhaps on the preprinted specific items) could be prepared for the various departments or divisions, and institutional, divisional, or departmental policy could specify which statistics and which formats are used for which audiences. Thus each audience would receive the data needed for its purposes in a form it finds congenial, but the instructor would control which, if any, outside audience receives data.

A unified program of this sort should be cost effective and acceptable to most faculty, administrators, and students. Problems that would have to be faced include selecting the precise items for the preprinted portions of the questionnaire, and the precise formats in which data would be reported; communicating to faculty the multipurpose nature of the program and convincing them that they do indeed control who has access to the information; and persuading review committees, administrators, and students that their needs are best served by three or fewer summary ratings.

In addition, the people responsible for a unified program would have to deal with an inherent tension between the informality and frequency of diagnostic evaluations and the formality and standardization of evaluations for personnel decisions and course selection. For example, in diagnostic evaluation it is often desirable to collect student or peer appraisals early, and perhaps repeatedly, so that problems can be discovered promptly and solutions tested; in personnel and course-selection evaluations, however, the data should probably be collected toward the end of the course and at approximately the same time in all comparable courses. Moreover, diagnostic data are most reasonably collected by the instructor and may involve dialogue even during the evaluation period, whereas personnel and course-selection data should probably be collected by someone else and should not involve, during the evaluation itself, dialogue between the students and the instructor. It would be truly unfortunate if the need for standardization in more formal evaluation discouraged or prohibited informal evaluation, especially early in the course. Possible solutions to this problem include allowing faculty to use the standard questionnaire occasionally, in addition to the formal evaluation period; preparing another form of the questionnaire that could be used outside the formal evaluation period; or simply urging faculty to do informal, diagnostic evaluation as often as they want by means of conversations and essay questionnaires that they themselves prepare.

An institutional evaluation office or resource center may play some role in a unified evaluation program depending on the scope of the program, the risks the institution is willing to take, and the institution's financial and educational priorities. The office's role might be limited to providing copies of preprinted questionnaires or a catalogue of evaluation items that instructors might use as the basis for their own questionnaires, documents such as the proposed instructor's guide to evaluation and the personnel-decisions handbook, and perhaps a bibliography of selected articles and books. In fact, for such limited services there is probably no reason why, once the materials have been prepared, they could not be supplied through the bookstore, library, storehouse, or other existing office, provided only that some arrangements are made for periodic review and revision of the materials and monitoring of the system. The materials could be provided free or for a fee, although experience indicates that charging a fee not only fails to encourage evaluation but actively discourages it.

A program of broader scope would provide data-processing services, that is, basic tabulation and cross-tabulation of ratings. The most difficult aspect of data processing is putting the questionnaire responses into a medium than can be computer tabulated. The options include keypunching, which produces the familiar computer card; key-to-tape, which is like cardpunching but produces a magnetic tape; optical scanning, in which a machine reads the penciled marks on special answer sheets; self-punching cards, in which the respondent uses a pencil tip or stylus to punch out perforated chad for a special computer card; and online processing, in which an operator uses a computer keyboard to enter the ratings directly into the computer. Which of these procedures an institution selects will depend on the institution's existing equipment and the net cost of the procedure in that particular institution. For institutions that prefer to purchase services from outside vendors, Centra (1979) lists some institutions and businesses that will contract to supply the necessary services for a fee. Local data-processing companies, too, may provide data-entry and tabulation services.

Computer programs to tabulate and report the data may be written locally, leased or borrowed from other institutions, or supplied through libraries of prepared programs. Locally written programs have the advantage of being designed to satisfy the needs of the local faculty; borrowed, leased, or purchased programs may include some special features not feasible in locally written programs. On the other hand, outside programs may be difficult to adapt to an institution's computers.

The risks that an institution takes by providing only the most limited support for evaluation are principally legal risks and risks that the evaluation program will be more symbolic than effective. Without considerable moral and policy support—not necessarily a great deal of financial support—it is unlikely that an evaluation program will operate safely within the continually changing requirements of law. Moreover, a program not treated seriously by administrators, faculty, and students is likely to grow loose and invite circumvention. Too little operational support may result in an inconvenient program that discourages use.

If an institution's financial and educational priorities permit, a full-service instructional evaluation and improvement office might be a worthwhile complement to the instructional program. Such an office would be staffed by full- or part-time professionals in instructional psychology and instructional evaluation with, for credibility and to attract the best staff, joint appointments as regular faculty in prestigious academic departments. Also for the sake of credibility, those staff members that specialize in course diagnosis and improvement should not be closely associated with the academic administration. The professional staff of such an office would not only prepare the questionnaires, item catalogues, instructor's guides, personnel-decisions handbooks, and bibliographies described above, but would also participate in the review of institutional policy for technical acceptability; consult with faculty and administrators about evaluation practice and the strengths and weaknesses of different approaches to evaluation; work with faculty as individuals or in small groups toward the improvement of teaching; keep faculty and administrators abreast of new developments; engage in research on instructional evaluation and improvement; and generally focus institutional attention on teaching. The nature and scope of professional-staff activities would be limited only by their creativity, energy, and expertise, and by the resources available.

18 Evaluating Evaluation Programs

The evaluation of evaluation programs is more a process than an event. Each step in the establishment of a program entails evaluation: determining the purpose of the evaluation, deciding on the focus, choosing the sources, constructing the instruments, collecting and reporting the data, and implementing, maintaining, and refining the program.

During the establishment process, evaluation is accomplished through committee deliberations, technical staff meetings, surveys, statistical analyses, and occasional experimental studies. These and other methods comprise what is essentially a formative evaluation, an evaluation for the purpose of shaping the program during its development. The establishment of most evaluation programs entails a considerable amount of formative evaluation for which many of the foregoing chapters have supplied guidelines and pertinent discussion.

Evaluation programs are less often subjected to summative evaluation, which is evaluation intended to produce a conclusion about the overall quality of the established program. The fundamental concept of summative evaluation is cost effectiveness and cost effectiveness is the focus of this chapter.

Effectiveness

Because effectiveness is the extent to which a program accomplishes what it is intended to accomplish, the effectiveness of an evaluation program must be measured in terms of the purpose of the evaluation.

Is an evaluation program effective at improving teaching? Indirect evidence in answer to this question can come from an analysis of the validity of the course and instructor characteristics the program measures and the reliability of the measures of those characteristics, but the most direct test is whether teaching does indeed improve as a result of participation in the program. The literature generally offers encouragement that participation in a student evaluation program can lead to better teaching as defined by increased student learning or, more often, by increased student ratings, and the result seems to be more favorable when the evaluation is communicated

151

to the instructor by a consultant or master teacher and when the student ratings are less favorable than the instructor's self-ratings (Root 1931, Centra 1972, Miller, 1971, Aleamoni 1974, Pambookian 1973, Centra 1973, Pambookian 1974, Doyle 1975, pp. 83–84). Neither peer nor self-evaluations have been studied in this regard, although reports of the effectiveness of peer evaluations are occasionally encountered (Clyde Parker, personal communication) and some degree of self- evaluation seems implicit in the use of any other form of evaluation for instructional improvement. Moreover, there seems to be no reason to expect that peer or self- evaluation would be any less effective at improving teaching than student evaluation, provided, as previously indicated, that the peers have had sufficient opportunity to observe what they are asked to evaluate.

But to ask if an evaluation program itself improves teaching is to pose a misleading question, for it implies passivity on the part of the instructor. Clearly a reliable and valid diagnostic-evaluation program can contribute to the improvement of teaching, but it will result in improvement only to the extent that the instructor is ready, willing, and able to change in response to the evaluation. Moreover, the difficulty of changing some instructional traits and behaviors argues for considerable patience in the assessment of change: habits developed over two or ten or twenty years are not likely to change in the few months that encompass the usual research design. Thus the encouraging results of the research so far reported are conservative: the actual effectiveness of the evaluation program studied may be greater than the data seem to show.

Is an evaluation program effective at improving personnel decisions? Personnel decisions are better to the extent that the proportion of correct decisions increases (Cronbach and Gleser 1965). Any personnel decision can be placed into one of four categories: correct affirmative, correct negative, incorrect affirmative, or incorrect negative. For example, a decision to award tenure would be placed in the correct-affirmative category if reliable and valid evidence demonstrated that the applicant had indeed surpassed all of the institution's criteria for tenure, and in the incorrect-affirmative category if not. A decision not to award tenure would belong in the correct-negative category if the evidence showed that the applicant had not met the criteria, in the incorrect-negative category if it showed that he or she had met them. An evaluation program intended to help improve personnel decisions should contribute to an increase in the proportion of correct-affirmative and correct-negative decisions and to a corresponding decrease in the proportion of incorrect-affirmative and incorrect-negative decisions.

The accuracy of decision making has been extensively studied in commerce and industry (see Cascio 1978, part IV) but it remains almost untouched in higher education. One reason for education's neglect of decision-making accuracy is said to be the complexity of the professorial role—and yet in business organizations there are managerial and executive positions that seem no less complex than that of teacher or teacher-researcher. A more compelling reason for the lack of attention to the accuracy of personnel decisions in higher education may be that only recently have budgetary restraints and the threat of litigation forced educators to become more attentive to personnel matters, and even under those conditions a technical approach to faculty-personnel decisions seems somehow incongenial, perhaps even an affront to the integrity and collegiality of academe.

For whatever reason, the literature is sparse with regard to the likelihood that an evaluation program might help to improve faculty-personnel decisions. The little research that has been published on the topic is mixed. Salthouse, McKeachie, and Lin's (1978) simulation study found that student evaluations had relatively little impact on recommendations for promotion or salary increase at a major university, perhaps, the authors suggest, because teaching itself was a relatively unimportant factor. On the other hand, Dornbush (1979) presents data that show that Stanford faculty and faculty at a variety of other very reputable schools wanted more attention paid to the evaluation (especially colleague evaluation) of teaching for personnel purposes, wanted the degree of evaluation more in proportion to the amount of time they put into the activity. There is thus at least a suggestion that more attention will be devoted to the improvement of personnel decisions based on teaching.

Despite this relative absence of research, logic and common sense dictate that evaluation of teaching for personnel decisions, like evaluation for formative and diagnostic purposes, can contribute to improved decisions so long as the questions asked are important and the answers given are reliable. Whether a personnel-evaluation program will lead to better decisions depends on the extent to which review committees and administrators are ready, willing, and able to use the data.

Is an evaluation program effective at improving course selection and program planning? There are several possible definitions of "better" course-selection decisions: an increased proportion in the number of students who learn to capacity, an increased proportion in the number who find the teaching satisfactory, and increased opportunity given for student learning by matching the course to the students' levels of ability and vocational, social, and cognitive development.

No data could be found that bear directly on the improvement of course-selection decisions under any of these definitions of effectiveness. Some indirect data do exist, however. For evaluations to be effective at improving course-selection decisions, the data must first be reliable and valid, as properly selected data are (chapters 5 and 11). The students must then pay attention to those data, which substantial numbers of them do (Coleman and McKeachie 1981, Hendel 1980). Finally, the students must be able

to follow the recommendation of these data—which may be the most difficult problem simply because work schedules, closed classes, distribution requirements, and other factors limit student freedom to choose courses.
Moreover, for those credits that are truly elective, student choice should be
at least as much determined by course content as by quality of teaching.
Thus the effectiveness of an evaluation program at improving course-selection decisions will be limited by the inability of students to use the data
fully. On the other hand, despite this limitation, the improvement of some
course-selection decisions on the part of some students may still be worth
the cost of the program. The next section of this chapter will address the
issue of program cost.

Cost

The costs of an educational program may be tangible or intangible, actual
or potential (Cronbach and Gleser 1965). The actual costs, tangible and
intangible, of establishing and maintaining an evaluation program include:

1. Faculty, administrator, student, and staff time given over to debating
    and planning the program.
2. Dollar costs of setting up the program: research and item selection.
3. Faculty, staff, administrator, and student costs in trying out the pro-
    gram: lost class time, diversion from other productive activities, any
    anxiety and annoyance.
4. Costs of operating the program: printing and distribution, data pro-
    cessing, colleague time for visiting classrooms and reviewing course
    materials, student time for filling out questionnaires and taking tests,
    and instructor and administrator time for interpreting the results.
5. Costs of evaluating the program: data collection and analysis, per-
    sonnel time for literature review, data interpretation, and deliberation.

In addition to these actual costs are certain very important potential
costs; for example:

1. The cost of incorrectly tenuring, or promoting, or otherwise rewarding
    an unsatisfactory teacher; for example, diminished collegiality, dimin-
    ished ability to recruit and retain the most desirable new faculty and
    students, general dissatisfaction and institutional embarrassment,
    diminished instructional quality, diminished quality of role-modeling
    for students and faculty.
2. The cost of incorrectly terminating, failing to promote, or otherwise
    failing to reward a good teacher: morale costs to students and faculty,

financial and professional harm to the faculty member in question; dollar costs, time costs, and anxiety and embarrassment associated with grievance and litigation.

3. The cost of incorrectly modifying (or not modifying) teaching in a course, or the cost of incorrect course choices: lessened student and instructor satisfaction, diminished opportunity for student learning, irritation and annoyance, diminished regard for evaluation.

Finally, because instructional decisions are made even in the absence of a formal evaluation program, or prior to the proposed revision of the existing program, the cost of operating the informal or existing program needs to be considered.

Cronbach and Gleser (1965, p. 24) present a complex yet—as they emphasize—still rudimentary formula for computing cost. More useful for present purposes might be a conceptual, subjective approach to the same end. To estimate the cost of a proposed new evaluation program or the cost of a major revision of an existing program, one should first, examine the actual and potential costs, tangible and intangible, of the new program or the revision; second, examine the actual and potential costs of the existing informal and unrevised program; then subtract the latter from the former to arrive at the net actual and potential, tangible and intangible, cost of the new program or the revision.

To estimate cost effectiveness, first estimate the new or revised program's probable net gain in effectiveness at making personnel, course-improvement, and course-selection decisions by subtracting the effectiveness of the existing program from the probable effectiveness of the new or revised program; then compare the net cost of the new or revised program to the net gain in effectiveness. This comparison will lead to an estimate of cost effectiveness.

Several principles should guide the comparison of net gain and net cost. Not surprisingly, one usually looks for a large gain in effectiveness at relatively small cost. More realistically, one may often have to be content with some increase in effectiveness at proportionately less increase in cost or, in especially hard times, a decrease in cost with little or no decrease in effectiveness. A slight increase in effectiveness can sometimes be worth considerable actual cost if the reduction of potential cost—for example, incorrect personnel decisions and consequent litigation—is great enough. Increases in actual costs, especially actual tangible costs—money costs—are seldom likely to be prohibitive unless an institution already has a demonstrably well-advanced evaluation program. (If actual, tangible costs are too high, they can often be reduced by minor changes in the proposed program or revision without unacceptable decrease in effectiveness or increase in potential cost.) Finally, costs should be considered over time, not only in the capitalization of initial expenses, but also with respect to the waxing and waning of such intangible costs as morale and faculty and student annoyance and anxiety. On the other hand, poorly estimated intangible costs may in the long run be more expensive to the institution than even substantial actual costs.

Cost-effectiveness principles are not only useful in decisions about establishing whole new programs or radically revising existing programs but also in decisions about the particulars of any program. For example, should the emphasis in a program be on personnel decisions, course improvement, or course selection? Historically, the emphasis has been on evaluation for course improvement—but the great potential costs of incorrect personnel decisions might indicate that this historical emphasis needs to change. Similarly, the increased emphasis on personnel decisions may justify the cost of more expensive rating methods such as forced-choice scaling. Should a program make use of both student and peer evaluation of classroom presentation? The traditional wisdom has been that, at least for important decisions, student evaluations should always be supplemented by other forms of evaluation. The anxiety and inconvenience of operating a classroom visitation program, however, coupled with the relative unreliability of peer evaluations of classroom teaching and the tendency of peers and students to rank instructors in much the same way might argue that peer visitation is not cost effective. Finally, sophisticated, computer-based systems with many different norms and advanced statistical analyses are aesthetically appealing (at least to evaluators), but unless these features bear on the usefulness of the data for the purposes at hand, their value might not readily justify their cost. Firm decisions of these sorts, however, need to be made in and by the institutions in which the programs operate.

In light of the sparse summative research on the effectiveness of personnel and course-selection evaluation programs, evaluators will either have to carry out their own studies of the effectiveness of these programs, wait until other investigators provide these studies, or rely on the foregoing argument that evaluation can improve these decisions. With regard to course-improvement evaluations, adequate data that these programs can work already seem to exist. In either case, the evaluation of evaluation programs ought to focus on the people for whose use the data are intended: on the extent to which instructors are (or how they can be persuaded or helped to become) ready, willing, and able to use diagnostic information in the improvement of their courses; or the extent to which review committees and administrators are or can become ready, willing, and able to use summary data in personnel decisions; and on the extent to which students and their academic advisors are or can become ready, willing, and able to use evaluations and course descriptions in program planning and course selection.

In this way research on the technical properties of an evaluation program, research on the overall effects of that program, and research on decision making itself all come together in the evaluation of instructional-evaluation programs.

Bibliography

Abrami, P.C.; Leventhal, L.; and Perry, R.P. 1982. Meta-analysis of research on educational seduction. American Educational Research Association Convention, New York.

Aleamoni, L.M. 1974. The usefulness of student evaluations improving college teaching. Urbana: University of Illinois Office of Instructional Resources, Measurement and Research Division.

American Psychological Association. 1966. *Standards for educational and psychological tests and manuals*. Washington, D.C.: American Psychological Association.

Anastasi, A. 1976. *Psychological testing*. 4th ed. New York: Macmillan.

Asch, S.E. 1956. Studies of independence and conformity. A minority of one against a unanimous majority. *Psychological Monographs* 70(9).

Astin, A.W., and Lee, C.B.T. 1966. Curent practices in the evaluation and training of college teachers. *Educational Record* 47:361-375.

Ausubel, D.P. 1968. *Educational psychology: A cognitive view*. New York: Holt, Rinehart and Winston.

Baker, B.O.; Hardyk, C.D.; and Petronovick, L.F. 1966. Weak measurement vs. strong statistics: An empirical critique of S.S. Stevens' proscriptions on statistics. *Educational and Psychological Measurement* 26:291-309.

Bejar, I.I., and Doyle, K.O., Jr. 1976a. Effect of prior expectations on the structure of student ratings of instruction. *Journal of Educational Measurement* 13(2).

———. 1976b. Students ratings of instruction: Expectations, first impressions, and evaluations. Minneapolis: University of Minnesota Measurement Services Center.

———. 1981. Factorial invariance in student ratings of instruction. *Applied Psychological Measurement* 5(3):307-312.

Berdie, D.R., and Anderson, J.F. 1974. *Questionnaires: Design and use*. Metuchen, N.J.: Scarecrow.

Berkowitz, H., and Zigler, E. 1965. Effects of preliminary positive and negative interactions and delay conditions on children's responsiveness to social reinforcement. *Journal of Personality and Social Psychology* 2:500-505.

Bieri, J.; Atkins, A.L.; Briar, S.; Leaman, R.L.; Miller, H.; and Tripodi, T. 1966. *Clinical and social judgment: The discrimination of behavioral information*. New York: Wiley.

Bloom, B.S.; Engelhart, M.B.; Furst, F.J.; Hill, W.H.; and Krathwohl,

D.R. 1956. *Taxonomy of educational objectives. Handbook I: Cognitive domain.* New York: Longmans Green.

Bolton, D.L. 1973. *Selection and evaluation of teachers.* Berkely, Calif.: McCutchen.

Borman, E.G., and Borman, N.C. 1972. *Effective small-group communication.* Minneapolis, Minn.: Burgess.

Borman, E.G.; Howell, W.F.; Nichols, R.G.; and Shapiro, G. 1982. Interpersonal communication in the modern organization. 2nd ed. Englewood Cliffs, N.J.: Prentice-Hall.

Borman, W.C. 1975. Effect of instructions to avoid halo error on reliability and validity of performance evaluation ratings. *Journal of Applied Psychology* 60:556-560.

———. 1978. Exploring the upper limits of reliability and validity in job performance ratings. *Journal of Applied Psychology* 63(2):135-144.

———. 1979. Format and training effects on rating accuracy and rater error. *Journal of Applied Psychology* 64(4):410-421.

Borman, W.C., and Vallon, W.R. 1974. A review of what can happen if behavioral expectation scales are developed in one setting and used in another. *Journal of Applied Psychology* 59:197-201.

Brascamp, L.A.; Ory, J.C.; and Pieper, D.M. 1981. Student written comments: Dimensions of instructional quality. *Journal of Educational Psychology* 73(1):65-70.

Brown, F.G. 1976. *Principles of educational and psychological testing.* New York: Holt, Rinehart and Winston.

Burris, R.; Keaton, R.; Landis, C.; and Park, R. 1979. *Teaching law with computers: A collection of essays.* Boulder, Colo.: Westview.

Campbell, D.T., and Fiske, D.W. 1959. Convergent and discriminant validation by the multitrait-multimethod matrix. *Psychological Bulletin* 56:81-105.

Campbell, J.P.; Dunnette, M.D.; Arvey, R.D.; and Hellervik, L.V. 1973. The development and evaluation of behaviorally based rating scales. *Journal of Applied Psychology* 57:15-22.

Carroll, J.D., and Chang, J.J. 1970. Analysis of individual differences in multi-dimensional scaling via an N-way generalization of "Eckart-Young" decomposition. *Psychometrika* 35:283-319.

Cascio, W.F. 1978. *Applied psychology in personnel management.* Reston, Va.: Reston.

Centra, J.A. 1972. Two studies of the utility of student ratings for improving teaching. Princeton, N.J.: Educational Testing Service. SIR Report No. 2.

———. 1973. Self ratings of college teachers: A comparison with student ratings. *Journal of Educational Measurement* 10(4):287-295.

———. 1974. The relationship between student and alumni ratings of teachers. *Educational and Psychological Measurement* 34(2):321–326.

———. 1975. Colleagues as raters of classroom instruction. *Journal of Higher Education* 46:327–337.

———. 1976. The influence of different directions on student ratings of instruction. *Journal of Educational Measurement* 13(4):277–282.

———. 1977. Student ratings of instruction and their relationship to-student learning. *American Educational Research Journal* 14(1): 17–24.

———. 1979. *Determining faculty effectiveness.* San Francisco: Jossey-Bass.

Church, A.T.; Trabin, T.; and Doyle, K.O., Jr. 1981. Student learning preferences and instructor evaluations. Minneapolis: University of Minnesota Measurement Services Center.

Cochran, W.C. 1977. *Sampling Techniques.* 3d ed. New York: Wiley.

Coffman, W. 1971. Essay examinations. In *Educational measurement,* R.L. Thorndike, ed. Washington, D.C.: American Council on Education.

Cohen, P. 1981. Student ratings of instruction and student achievement: A meta-analysis of multisection validity studies. *Review of Educational Research* 51(3):281–309.

Cohen, S.H., and Berger, W.G. 1970. Dimensions of students' ratings of college instructors underlying subsequent achievement on course examinations. *Proceedings,* 78th Annual Convention, American Psychological Association:605–606.

Coleman, J.S. 1961. *The adolescent society.* New York: Free Press.

Coleman, J., and McKeachie, W.J. 1981. Effects of instructor/course evaluations on student course selection. *Journal of Educational Psychology* 73(2):224–226.

Costin, F.; Greenough, W.T.; and Menges, R.J. 1971. Student ratings of college teaching: Reliability, validity and usefulness. *Review of Educational Research* 41:411–535.

Crichton, L.I., and Doyle, K.O., Jr. 1976a. Models for the reliability of stimulus ratings. Minneapolis: University of Minnesota Measurement Services Center.

———. 1976b. Statistical procedures for estimating the reliability of stimulus ratings. Minneapolis: University of Minnesota Measurement Services Center.

Crittenden, K.S., and Norr, J.L. 1974. Student values and teacher evaluation: A problem in person perception. *Sociometry* 36:143–151.

Crockett, W.H. 1975. Impressions of a speaker as a function of set to understand or to evaluate, of cognitive complexity, and of prior attitudes. *Journal of Personality* 43:168–178.

Cronbach, L.J. 1957. The two disciplines of scientific psychology. *American Psychologist* 12:671–684.

———. 1967. How can instruction be adapted to individual differences? In R.M. Gagné *Learning and individual differences.* Columbus, Ohio: Merrill.

———. 1975. Beyond the two disciplines of scientific psychology. *American Psychologist* 30:116–127.

Cronbach, L.J., and Gleser, G.C. *Psychological Tests and Personnel Decisions.* 1965. 2nd ed. Urbana: University of Illinois Press.

Cronbach, L.J.; Gleser, G.C.; Nanda, H.; and Rajaratnam, N. 1972. *The Dependability of behavioral measurements.* New York: Wiley.

Cronbach, L.J., and Meehl, P.E. 1955. Construct validity in psychological tests. *Psychological Bulletin* 52:281–302.

Cronbach, L.J., and Snow, R.E. 1977. *Aptitudes and instructional methods.* New York: Irvington.

Curran, C.A. 1972. *Counseling-learning: A whole-person model for education.* New York: Grune and Stratton.

Derry, J.O., and the Staff of the Measurement and Research Center. 1974. The cafeteria system: A new approach to course and instructor evaluation. Lafayette, Ind.: Purdue University Measurement and Research Center. Institutional Research Bulletin:74–1.

de Wolf, V.A. 1974. *Student ratings of instruction in post-secondary institutions: A comprehensive annotated bibliography of research reported since 1968.* Seattle: University of Washington Bureau of Testing.

Domino, G. 1971. Interactive effects of achievement orientation and teaching style on academic achievement. *Journal of Educational Psychology* 62:427–431.

Dornbush, S.M. 1979. Perspectives from sociology: Organizational evaluation of faculty performances. In D.R. Lewis and W.E. Becker, *Academic rewards in higher education.* Cambridge, Mass.: Ballinger.

Doyle, K.O., Jr. 1972. Construction and evaluation of scales for rating college instructors. Unpublished doctoral dissertation. University of Minnesota. *Dissertation Abstracts International,* 33(5-A):2163.

———. 1975. *Student Evaluation of Instruction.* Lexington, Mass.: D.C. Heath.

———. 1977. Psychometrics and psychoanalysis: *Extrema se tangunt.* Minneapolis: University of Minnesota Measurement Services Center.

———. 1979. Use of student evaluations in faculty personnel decisions. In D.R. Lewis and W.E. Becker, eds. *Academic Rewards in Higher Education.* Cambridge, Mass.: Ballinger.

———. 1980. An abecedary of sampling. *New directions for institutional advancement.* San Francisco: Jossey-Bass.

Doyle, K.O., Jr., and Bejar, I.I. 1973. Computer-generated narrative-format instructor-assistance classroom-data reports. *American Educational Research Association Convention*, New Orleans.

Doyle, K.O., Jr. and Crichton, L. 1978. Student, peer, and self evaluations of college instructors. *Journal of Educational Psychology,* 70:815–826.

Doyle, K.O., Jr., and Moen, R.E. 1978. Toward the definition of a domain of academic motivation. *Journal of Educational Psychology* 70(2):231–236.

Doyle, K.O., Jr., and Wattawa, S. 1977. Programs for the construction and analysis of custom questionnaires. *Educational and Psychological Measurement* 37(2):237–239.

Doyle, K.O., Jr., and Webber, P.L. 1978*a*. Self and student ratings of instruction. Minneapolis: University of Minnesota Measurement Services Center.

———. 1978b. Self ratings of college instruction. *American Educational Research Journal* 15(3):467–475.

Doyle, K.O., Jr., and Whitely, S.E. 1974. Student ratings as criteria for effective teaching. *American Educational Research Journal* 11(3): 259–274.

Drucker, A.J., and Remmers, H.H. 1951. Do alumni and students differ in their attitudes toward instructors? *Journal of Educational Psychology* 42:129–143.

Duncan, M.J., and Biddle, B.J. 1974. *The study of teaching.* New York: Holt, Rinehart and Winston.

Ebel, K.E. 1972. *The recognition and evaluation of teaching.* Washington, D.C.: American Association of University Professors Project to Improve College Teaching.

Elliott, D.H. 1950. Characteristics and relationships of various criteria of college and university teaching. *Purdue University Studies in Higher Education,* 70:5–61.

Feldman, K.A. 1977. Consistency and variability among college students in rating their teachers and courses: A review and analysis. *Research in Higher Education* 6(3):223–274.

Flanagan, J.C. 1954. The critical incident technique. *Psychological Bulletin* 51:327–358.

Freud, S. 1914. *Psychopathology of everyday life.* In *The writings of Sigmund Freud.* A.A. Brill, ed. New York: Modern Library, 1938.

Frey, P.W. 1973. Student ratings of teaching: Validity of several rating factors. *Science* 182:83–85.

———. 1976. Validity of student instructional ratings: Does timing matter? *Journal of Higher Education* 47:327–336.

Gage, N.L. 1958. Ends and means in appraising college training. *Conference on Appraisal of Teaching in Large Universities.* University of Michigan, Ann Arbor.

Gage, N.L., and Berliner, D.C. 1975. *Educational psychology.* Chicago: Rand McNally.

Gagné, F., and Allaire, D. 1974. Summary of research data on the reliability and validity of a measure of satisfaction derived from Reality-Desires discrepancies. Quebec: Institute National de la Recherche Scientifique, Université de Québec.

Gagné, R.M. 1970. *The Conditions of learning.* 2nd ed. New York: Holt, Rinehart and Winston.

Ghiselli, E.E. 1956. Dimensional problems of criteria. *Journal of Applied Psychology* 40:1-4.

Ghiselli, E.E., and Ghiselli, W.B. 1972. Ratings—*kundgabe* or *beschreibung. Journal of Psychology* 80:263-271.

Gillmore, G.M.; Kane, M.T.; and Naccarato, R.W. 1978. The generalizability of student ratings of instruction: Estimation of teacher and course components. *Journal of Educational Measurement* 15(1)1-13.

Glass, G. 1974. In H.J. Wahlberg, ed., *Evaluating educational performance.* Berkeley, Calif.: McCutchen.

Glass, G.V. 1976. Primary, secondary, and meta-analysis of research. *Educational Researcher* 5:3-8.

Grasha, A.F. 1977. *Assessing and developing faculty performance.* Cincinnati, Ohio: Communication and Education Associates.

Gronlund, N.E. 1981. *Measurement and evaluation in teaching.* 4th ed. New York: Macmillan.

Guilford, J.P. 1954. *Psychometric methods.* New York: McGraw-Hill.

Hakel, M. 1969. Significance of implicit personality theories for personality research and theory. *Preceedings,* 77th Annual Meeting of the American Psychological Association. Washington, D.C.: American Psychological Association.

Hansen, M.H.; Hurwitz, W.N.; and Madow, E.G. 1953. *Sample survey methods and theory.* vol. 1: *Methods and applications.* vol. 2: *Theory.* New York: Wiley.

Harvey, O.J.; Hunt, D.E.; and Schroeder, H.M. 1961. *Conceptual systems and personality organization.* New York: Wiley.

Heider, F. 1958. *The Psychology of Interpersonal relations.* New York: Wiley.

Hendel, D.D. 1980. Evaluation of the pilot project for the Student Course Information Project. Minneapolis: University of Minnesota Measurement Services Center.

Hildebrand, M.; Wilson, R.C.; and Dienst, E.R. 1971. *Evaluating university teaching.* Berkeley: University of California Center for Research and Development in Higher Education.

Horton, D.C., and Turnage, T.W. 1976. *Human learning.* Englewood Cliffs, N.J.: Prentice-Hall.

Howard, G.S.; Ralph, K.M; Gulanick, N.A.; Maxwell, S.E.; Nance, D.W.; and Gerber, S.K. 1979. Internal invalidity in pretest-posttest self report evaluations and a re-evaluation of retrospective pretests. *Applied Psychological Measurement* 3(1):1–23.

ICES. 1977. Instructor and Course Evaluation System. Urbana-Champaign: University of Illinois Office of Instructional Resources.

Isaacson, R.L.; McKeachie, W.J.; Milholland, J.E.; Lin, Y.G.; Hofeller, M; Baerwaldt, J.W.; and Zinn, K.L. 1964. Dimensions of student evaluations of teaching. *Journal of Educational Psychology* 55(6):344–351.

James, W. 1890. *Principles of psychology.* New York: Holt.

Johnson, D.W., and Johnson, R.T. 1975. *Learning together and alone: Cooperation, competition, and individualization.* Englewood Cliffs, N.J.: Prentice-Hall.

Joyce, B., and Weil, M. 1972. *Models of teaching.* Englewood Cliffs, N.J.: Prentice-Hall.

Kaplan, W.A. 1978. *The Law of higher education: Legal implications of administrative decision making.* San Francisco: Jossey-Bass.

Kavanaugh, M.J.; MacKinney, A.C.; and Wolins, L. 1971. Issues in managerial performance: Multitrait-multimethod analysis of ratings. *Psychological Bulletin* 75:34–49.

Kelly, G.A. 1955. *The psychology of personal constructs.* New York: Norton.

Kent, L. 1966. Student evaluation of teaching. *Educational Record* 47(3): 376–406.

Kiresuk, T.J., and Sherman, R.E. 1968. Goal attainment scaling: A general method for evaluating comprehensive community mental health programs. *Community Mental Health Journal* 4(6):443–453.

Kish, L. 1965. *Survey sampling.* New York: Wiley.

Kramer, S.N. 1963. *The sumerians.* Chicago: University of Chicago Press.

Krathwohl, D.R.; Bloom, B.S.; and Masia, B.B. 1964. *Taxonomy of educational objectives. Handbook II: Affective domain.* New York: McKay.

Kratz, H.E. 1896. Characteristics of the best teachers as recognized by children. *Pedagogical Seminar* 3:413–418.

Kulik, J.A., and McKeachie, W.J. 1975. The evaluation of teachers in higher education. In *Review of Research in Education, Vol. 3,* F.N. Kerlenger, ed. Itasca: Ill.: Peacock.

LaForge, R. 1965. Components or reliability. *Psychometrika* 30:187–195.

Lenning, O.T. 1977. *A structure for the outcomes of postsecondary education.* Boulder, Colo.: National Center for Higher Education Management Systems.

Leventhal, L. 1975. Teacher rating forms: Critique and reformulation of previous validation studies. *Canadian Psychological Review* 16:260–276.

Levinthal, C.F.; Lansky, L.M.; and Andrews, O.E. 1971. Student evaluations of teacher behaviors as estimations of real-ideal discrepancies: A critique of teacher rating methods. *Journal of Educational Psychology* 62:104–109.

Lott, A.J., and Lott, B.E. 1966. Group cohesiveness and individual learning. *Journal of Educational Psychology* 57:61–73.

Lovell, G.D., and Haner, C.F. 1955. Forced-choice scales applied to college faculty rating. *Educational and Psychological Measurement* 15:291–304.

Maier, N.R.F. 1952. *Principles of human relations.* New York: Wiley.

Marsh, H.W., and Hocevar, D. 1980. An application of LISREL modeling to multitrait-multimethod analysis. Paper presented at the Annual Meeting of the Australian Association for Research in Education, Sydney.

Marsh, H.W., and Overall, J.U. n.d. Validity of students' evaluations of teaching: A comparison with instructor self evaluations by teaching assistants, undergraduate faculty and graduate faculty. Los Angeles: University of Southern California Office of Institutional Studies.

Marsh, H.W.; Overall, J.U.; and Kessler, S.P. 1979. Validity of student evaluations of instructional effectiveness: A comparison of faculty self evaluations and evaluations by their students. *Journal of Educational Psychology* 71:149–160.

Massey, B. ed. 1975. *Proceedings. Heidelberg: International Conference on Improving University Teaching.*

McGuire, C.H., and Babbott, D. 1967. Simulation technique in the measurement of problem-solving skills. *Journal of Educational Measurement* 4, 1–10.

McKeachie, W.J. 1978. *Teaching tips,* 7th ed. Lexington, Mass.: D.C. Heath.

McKeachie, W.J., and Lin, Y.G. 1971. Sex differences in student response to college teachers: Teacher warmth and teacher sex. *American Educational Research Journal* 8:221–226.

McKeachie, W.J.; Lin, Y.G.; and Mann, W. 1971. Student ratings of teacher effectiveness: Validity studies. *American Educational Research Journal* 8:435–445.

McNemar, Q. 1969. *Psychological statistics.* 4th ed. New York: Wiley.

Mehrens, W.A., and Lehmann, I.J. 1978. *Measurement and evaluation in education and psychology,* 2nd ed. New York: Holt, Rinehart and Winston.

Messick, S. (1970.) The criterion problem in the evaluation of instruction: Assessing possible, not just intended, outcomes. In *The evaluation of instruction: Issues and problems,* M.C. Wittrock and D.E. Wiley, eds. New York: Holt, Rinehart and Winston.

Miller, M.T. 1971. Instructor attitudes toward, and their use of, student ratings of teachers. *Journal of Educational Psychology* 62:235–239.

Miller, R.I. 1972. *Evaluating faculty performance.* San Francisco: Jossey-Bass.

———. 1974. *Developing programs for faculty evaluation.* San Francisco: Jossey-Bass.

Millman, J., ed. 1981. *Handbook of teacher evaluation.* Beverly Hills: Sage.

Milton, O. 1982. *Will that be on the final?* Springfield, Ill.: Thomas.

Moen, R.E. 1978. Toward the measurement of academic motivations. Unpublished doctoral dissertation, University of Minnesota. *Dissertation Abstracts International* 39/09:54 16–A.

Moen, R.E., and Doyle, K.O., Jr. 1977. Construction and development of the Academic Motivations Inventory (AMI). *Educational and Psychological Measurement* 37:509–512.

Morsh, J.E., and Wilder, E.W. 1954. Identifying the effective instructor: A review of quantitative studies, 1900–1952. San Antonio: Tex.: AFPTRC Research Bulletin, Air Force Personnel and Training Research Center, Lackland AFB.

Moser, C.A., and Karlton, G. 1972. *Survey methods in social investigation.* New York: Basic Books.

Nunnally, J.C. 1967. *Psychometric theory.* New York: McGraw-Hill.

Oppenheim, A.N. 1966. *Questionnaire design and attitude measurement.* New York: Basic Books.

Ory, J.C.; Brascamp, L.A.; and Piepen, D.M. 1980. Consistency of student evaluation information collected by three methods. *Journal of Educational Psychology* 72(2):181–185.

Overall, J.E. 1965. Reliability of composite ratings. *Educational and Psychological Measurement* 25:1011–1012.

Packer, J., and Bain, J.D. 1978. Cognitive style and teacher-student compatibility. *Journal of Educational Psychology* 70:864–871.

Page, C.F. 1974. *Student evaluation of teaching: The American experience.* Society for Research into Higher Education.

Pambookian, H.S. 1973. The effect of feedback from students to college instructors on their teaching behavior. Unpublished doctoral dissertation, University of Michigan. *Dissertation Abstracts International* 33(9–A):4950.

———. 1974. Initial level of student evaluation of instruction as a source of instructor change after feedback. *Journal of Education Psychology* 66:52–56.

Parent, E.R.; Vaughan, C.E.; and Wharton, K. 1971. A new approach to course evaluation. *Journal of Higher Education* 42(2):133–138.

Parker, C.A., and Lawson, J.M. 1978. From theory to practice to theory: Consulting with college faculty. *Personnel and Guidance Journal* 56(7): 424–427.

Perry, W.G. 1968. *Forms of intellectual and ethical development in the college years: A schema.* New York: Holt, Rinehart and Winston.

Remmers, H.H.; Martin, F.D.; and Elliott, D.N. 1949. Are students ratings of instructors related to their grades? *Purdue University Studies in Higher Education* 66:17–26.

Root, A.R. 1931. Student ratings of teachers. *Journal of Higher Education* 2:311–315.

Rosenshine, B. 1971. *Teaching behaviors and student achievement.* London: National Foundation for Educational Research in England and Wales.

Saal, F.E.; Downey, R.G.; and Lahey, M.A. 1980. Rating the ratings: Assessing the psychometric quality of rating data. *Psychological Bulletin* 83(2):413–428.

Salthouse, T.A.; McKeachie, W.J.; and Lin, Y.G. 1978. An experimental investigation of factors affecting university promotion decisions. *Journal of Higher Education* 49:177–183.

Schachter, S. 1967. In *Neurophysiology and emotion,* D.C. Glass, ed. New York: Rockefeller University Press and Russell Sage Foundation.

Schneider, D.J. 1973. Implicit personality theory: A review. *Psychological Bulletin* 79:294–309.

Schwab, D.P.; Henneman, H.G.; and DeCotiis, T.A. 1975. Behaviorally anchored rating scales: A review of the literature. *Personnel Psychology* 28:549–562.

Scriven, M. 1981. Summative teacher evaluation. In *Handbook of teacher evaluation,* J. Millman ed. Beverly Hills: Sage.

Seldin, P. 1980. *Successful faculty evaluation programs.* Crugers, N.Y.: Coventry.

Sharon, A.T. 1970. Eliminating bias from student ratings of college instructors. *Journal of Applied Psychology* 54:278–281.

Sharon, A.T., and Bartlett, C.J. 1969. Effect of instructional conditions in producing leniency on two types of rating scales. *Personnel Psychology* 22:251–263.

Shulman, L.S., and Tamir, P. 1973. Research on teaching in the natural sciences. In *Second handbook of research and teaching,* R.M.W. Travers, ed. Chicago: Rand McNally.

Siegel, S. 1956. *Non-parametric statistics.* New York: McGraw-Hill.

Skinner, B.F. 1968. *The technology of teaching.* New York: Appleton-Century-Crofts.

Smith, P.C., and Kendall, J.G. 1963. Retranslation of expectations: An approach to the construction of unambiguous anchoring of rating scales. *Journal of Applied Psychology* 47:149–155.

Sockloff, A.L., ed. 1973. *Proceedings: First invitational conference on faculty effectiveness as evaluated by students.* Philadelphia: Temple University Measurement and Research Center.

Stanley, J. 1971. Reliability. In *Educational Measurement,* R.L. Thorndike, ed. Washington, D.C.: American Council on Education.

Starry, A.R.; Derry, J.O.; and Wright, G.L. 1973. An automated instructor and course appraisal system. *Educational Technology* 13:61–64.

Stone, E.F.; Spool, M.D.; and Rabinowitz, S. 1977. Effect of anonymity on student evaluations of faculty performance. *Research in Higher Education* 6:313–325.

Sudman, S. 1976. *Applied sampling.* New York: Academic Press.

Sullivan, A.M., and Skanes, G.R. 1974. Validity of student evaluation of teaching and characteristics of successful instructors. *Journal of Educational Psychology* 66:584–590.

Sweet, W. 1968. *Artes Latinae.* Chicago: Encyclopaedia Britannica Films.

Tellegen, A. 1976. Differential personality questionnaire. Unpublished manuscript. Minneapolis: University of Minnesota Department of Psychology.

Thorndike, R.L. 1967. Reliability. In *Problems in human assessment,* D.N. Jackson and S. Messick, eds. New York: McGraw-Hill, 1967.

Thorndike, R.L., ed. 1971. *Educational measurement.* Washington, D.C.: American Council on Education.

Trabin, T., and Doyle, K.O., Jr. 1981. Measures of cognitive structure as predictors of variability in student ratings. Minneapolis: University of Minnesota Measurement Services Center.

Trent, J.W., and Cohen, A.M. 1973. Research on teaching in higher education. In *Second handbook of research on teaching,* R.M.W. Travers ed. Chicago: Rand McNally.

Truax, C.G., and Carkhuff, R.R. 1967. *Toward effective counseling and psychotherapy.* Chicago: Aldine.

Tucker, L.R., and Messick, S. 1963. An individual differences model for multi-dimensional scaling. *Psychometrika* 28:333–367.

Ullian, J., and Parker, C.A. 1980. Teaching improvement consultants: Biennial project report 1978–80. Minneapolis: University of Minnesota Department of Social, Psychological and Philosophical Foundations of Education.

Uranowitz, S., and Doyle, K.O., Jr. 1978. Being liked and teaching: The bases and effects of personal likeability in college instruction. *Research in Higher Education* 9.

Verderber, R.F. 1976. *The challenge of effective speaking.* 3rd ed. Belmont, Calif.: Wadsworth.

Walden, J.W.H. 1909. *Universities of ancient Greece.* New York: Scribner's.

Ward, M.D.; Clark, D.C.; and Von Harrison, G. 1981. The observer effect in classroom visitation. American Educational Research Association Convention, Los Angeles.

Weiss, D.J. 1970. Factor analysis and counseling research. *Journal of Counseling Psychology* 17:477–485.

Weiss, D.J. forthcoming. Adaptive testing. *International Encyclopedia of Education.* Oxford: Pergamon.

Weiss, D.J., and Davidson, M. 1981. Test theory and methods. *Annual Review of Psychology* 32:629–658.

Werdell, P.R. 1967. *Course and teacher evaluation,* 2nd ed. Washington, D.C.: United States National Student Association.

Wesman, A.G., 1971. Writing the test item. In *Educational measurement,* R.L. Thorndike, ed. Washington, D.C.: American Council on Education.

Wherry, R.J. 1952. Control of bias in ratings. Department of the Army, Adjutant General's Office, Personnel Research and Procedures Division, Personnel Research Branch. PRS Reports 914, 915, 919, 920, 921.

Whitely, S.E., and Doyle, K.O., Jr. 1976a. Implicit theories in student ratings. *American Educational Research Journal* 13(4):241–253.

———. 1978. Dimensions of effective teaching: Factors or artifacts? *Educational and Psychological Measurement* 38:107–117.

———. 1979. Validity and generalizability of student ratings from between-class and within-class data. *Journal of Educational Psychology* 71(1):117–124.

Whitely, S.E., Doyle, K.O., Jr., and Hopkinson, K. 1973. Student ratings and criteria for effective teaching. Minneapolis: University of Minnesota Measurement Services Center.

Wiener, P. 1982. Ratings Blindfold: Forced-choice methodology and applications from 1933 to 1980. Minneapolis: University of Minnesota Department of Social, Psychological, and Philosophical Foundations of Education.

Witkin, H.A. 1976. Cognitive style in academic performance and in teacher-student relations. In *Individuality in Learning,* S. Messick et al. San Francisco: Jossey-Bass.

Wittrock, M.C., and Lumsdaine, A.A. 1977. *Instructional psychology. Annual Review of Psychology* 28:417–459.

Wright, R.J., and Richardson, L. 1977. The effect of response style on cognitive complexity and course evaluation. *Educational and Psychological Measurement* 37:177–183.

Index

About the Author

Kenneth O. Doyle, Jr., studied literature and languages at Mount St. Paul College and philosophy at the Pontifical Gregorian University, receiving the A.B. from Marquette University and the Ph.D. from the University of Minnesota. Since 1972 he has been research associate in the Measurement Services Center, University of Minnesota, in charge of the instructional evaluation and testing divisions. He is author and co-author of numerous papers on the conceptual and psychometric aspects of instructional evaluation, editor of *Interaction: Readings in Human Psychology* (D.C. Heath and Company, 1973), co-compiler of *A Scholar's Guide to Education/ Psychology Journals,* and author of *Student Evaluation of Instruction* (D.C. Heath and Company, 1975). A recipient of the Palmer Johnson award for research on instructional evaluation, he has been co-chairman of the American Educational Research Association Special Interest Group on Instructional Evaluation and of the Committee on Institutional Cooperation Panel on Faculty Evaluation and Development. In addition, he is a consultant on personnel and institutional evaluation and research methodology and is engaged in private practice.